More
AND STILL
More

A PASSION FOR ALL GOD OFFERS

Joe Engelk

D1507931

Pacific Press® Publishing Association
Nampa, Idaho
Oshawa, Ontario, Canada

Edited by Kenneth R. Wade
Designed by Michelle C. Petz
Wheatfield image copyright © 1997 PhotoDisc, Inc.

Copyright © 1998 by
Pacific Press® Publishing Association
Printed in the United States of America
All Rights Reserved

ISBN 0-8163-1710-0

98 99 00 01 02 • 5 4 3 2 1

Table of Contents

Dedication

to Delinda Snyder and Philip Baptiste
in gratitude for their prayer-filled leadership
at many prayer and ministry conferences
and to the Spirit-filled youth
whom God is raising up in every nation on earth.

Introduction

Everything God Offers

"I promise that I'll bless you with everything I have—
bless and bless and bless!"
(Hebrews 6:14, The Message)

"Anything God has done in the past He is able to duplicate or exceed," Wesley L. Duewel wrote in his book *Mighty Prevailing Prayer*. "He is forever the same in wisdom, love, and power" (page 12).

An example from Exodus:

- God took a spoiled prince in Egypt and transformed him into a humble leader whom He used to deliver two million slaves.

Two examples from Acts:

- God led 120 upper-room believers to put away their differences, draw close to Him and each other, and then go out and turn the world upside down.
- God took Saul, a persecutor of the early church, and transformed him into the Paul who wrote thirteen of the epistles of the New Testament, along with taking the gospel to tens of thousands of Gentiles.

All the preceding changes involved the kind of miracle God most longs to perform today—restyling people into loyal, godly reflections of Himself. One message from heaven put it this way: "The eyes of the Lord run to and fro throughout the whole earth, to show Himself strong on behalf of those whose heart is loyal to Him" (2 Chronicles 16:9).*

The preceding words, first spoken by a prophet to King Asa of Judah, describe what God is up to as we approach a new millennium. He is looking for loyal, fully committed youth and leaders and laymen who *really believe* that what He has done in the past in changing lives He is able to duplicate and exceed today. Then, through a committed, godly people, He intends that the eternal gospel of Revelation 14 go to "every nation, tribe, tongue, and people" (Revelation 14:6).

OBJECTIVES FOR THIS BOOK

This book has been written to:

- Help inspire and nurture those who have joined the Seventh-day Adventist Church through the influence of NET '98 and other forms of evangelism.
- Help bring about an ever-increasing interest in prayer, Bible study, and witnessing.
- Motivate all of us to seek the qualities of character found in our precious Savior.

In a class at Andrews University that we call Workshop in Prayer, students underline eighty of the better known Old Testament promises, eighty New Testament promises, and fifty command promises. On the first day of underlining I always include God's Genesis 12:2 promise to Abraham: "I will bless you . . . and you shall be a blessing."

"This promise is for us just as much as for Abraham," I tell students. I write on the board the Hebrews 6:14 paraphrase cited at the start of this introduction and add, "Notice the *everything I have!* God did that at Calvary, not just for Abraham, but for each of us. 'All of heaven, all in one, God gave us all when He gave His Son.' "

"He didn't stop at Calvary," I add. "God wants to give us, individually and collectively, every spiritual blessing the Bible offers—more love, more humility, a deeper repentance, more joy, more faith, more and more *of everything prom-ised!*"

BLESSINGS THAT CAN BECOME OURS

In my classes we always memorize several Bible prayers. Often we start with this prayer of Paul for the Philippians:

> This I pray, that your love may abound still more and more in knowledge and all discernment, that you may approve the things that are excellent, that you may be sincere and without offense till the day of Christ, being filled with the fruits of righteousness which are by Jesus Christ to the glory and praise of God (Philippians 1:9-11).

I used the preceding prayer as the theme for the first book of this series, *30 Days to a More Powerful Prayer Life*. In this second book my purpose is to ex-plore samples of the blessings that can become ours, as the above passage puts it, by "being filled with the fruits of righteousness which are by Jesus Christ to the praise and glory of God."

As he told about Christ's earthly ministry, John said that God gave Jesus "the fullness of his Spirit" (John 3:34, TEV). A "measureless" amount, says the New English Bible. "Without limit," according to the New International Version.

> The heart that has once tasted the love of Christ cries out continually for a deeper draft, and as you impart you will receive in richer and more abundant measure. Every revelation of God to the soul increases the ca-pacity to know and to love. The continual cry of the heart is, "More of Thee," and ever the Spirit's answer is, "Much more" (*Thoughts From the Mount of Blessing*, page 20).

This book deals with the *how tos* for entering into that kind of experience. But first, an example of what God can do.

MARLA'S STORY

In the February 1998 NAD edition of the *Adventist Review*, Roy Adams told about a remarkable Black woman in her late thirties. God has helped her become one of the ten judges in Monterey County, California. As she entered the career arena, she faced three obstacles to reaching a high position—she's Black, a woman, and still relatively young.

Her parents, Wendall and Cora Osborne, had immigrated to the United States from Panama. They came so their girls could have access to the best possible Christian education. (A son, their oldest child, had remained in Panama to finish high school.)

Marla was born in 1959 at the Hadley Memorial Hospital in Washington, D.C. When she was old enough for school, the Adventist school to which they applied would, at that time, admit only a certain quota of Blacks. The school had admitted her older sisters, but Marla had to wait until third grade to get in.

In concluding his report, the author cited these words from Judge Anderson: "So far in my life , I've left it up to God. And that's been the best thing, because I'm today where I couldn't even dream. And I think that is how I will continue the rest of my life. Whatever I can dream is nothing close to what God dreams for me."

She then added: "So as long as I listen to God's voice, then I'll be where I can't even imagine."

Christ once pointed to a grapevine and said, "In the same way that a branch can't bear grapes by itself but only by being joined to the vine, you can't bear fruit unless you are joined with me. I am the Vine, you are the branches. When you are joined with me and I with you . . . the harvest is sure to be abundant" (John 15:4, 5, The Message).

In the chapter "A Higher Experience" the author of *The Ministry of Healing* points out, "All power, all wisdom, are at our command. . . . With the power and light that God imparts, you can comprehend more and accomplish more than you ever before deemed possible" (page 514).

If you scanned the table of contents, you've noticed that many titles in this book include the word *passion*. According to Webster it originally meant suffering or agony, as in Christ's final week on earth. Other current meanings include any strong emotion or desire, or a fondness, as in a passion for music. Synonyms include fervor, ardor, enthusiasm, and zeal.

BLESSINGS AND SURPRISES

In a report in the *Adventist Review*, July 1998 North American edition, Monte Sahlin said this about the 15,000 who joined the Seventh-day Adventist Church during NET '95 and NET '96:

- Ninety percent are still active members of the church.
- Nearly half (47 percent) are already integrated into the ministries of the local church.
- In gender 48 percent of these members are male and 52 percent are females.
- The majority are under forty-five years of age.
- With NET '95, nearly half reported that a friend, relative, or acquaintance invited them to the meetings.

These are good reasons to become passionate about sharing our faith, and for expecting more and more and still more!

This book, like *30 Days*, includes testimonies about my own experience, mostly over the last few months. I am also including the experiences of several Andrews University students who have been involved in prayer and ministry activities.

In what you are about to read, each chapter begins with a Bible statement. The close of each chapter will include ideas from the chapter that you can think of as possible "I can test this" options.

In chapter 1 we look at how prayer helps move us into "miracle territory."

———————

* Unless otherwise stated all Scripture quotations are from the New King James Version.

Chapter 1

Miracle Territory

"Ask, and it will be given to you; seek, and you will find; knock, and it will be opened to you."
(Luke 11:9)

Are you and I asking and seeking and knocking like we *really, really believe* the preceding promise? "Prayer," H. M. S. Richards, the founder of the Voice of Prophecy, once said, "is the most talked about and least practiced of all Christian beliefs."

Pastor Dwight Nelson, the speaker for NET '98, and pastor of the Pioneer Memorial Church, has repeatedly given messages and series of messages about prayer. At the time of this writing, six months before NET '98 begins, he's been doing a series titled "A Stubborn Passion." In the first message, "My Friend Harry," he told about an Andrews University doctoral student from Africa who regularly comes to his office to pray for and with him.

"When Harry starts talking to me," Pastor Dwight said, "we are not sixty seconds into our conversation before he will explode with his passion for lost people. Then we will kneel and pray together, and when we are through, I am ready to turn in my keys and join him as an itinerant preacher out to win every man, woman, and child on earth."

In his sermon series, Pastor Dwight dealt with two basic themes—a passion for lost people, and a passion to pray for them.

A PASSION FOR PRAYER

I see evidence, especially among Adventist youth, that through prayer and ministry conferences, *prayer without passion* is becoming a *passion for prayer*. And with that passion God is bringing a passion for other good things such as Bible study and ministry.

For readers not acquainted with the term, a prayer conference is an experience where those who attend spend one to three days, within the context of small groups, taking part in three basic activities: prayer, Bible study, and ministry.

The first such conference among Adventists was held in Oregon in 1988. By 1995 there were thirteen, there were sixty-five in 1996, and eighty-five in 1997. In the preceding paragraph I call such sessions an *experience*—something that involves *personal participation*. Most of the time at a prayer conference that's what people get: actual experience in meaningful Bible study and prayer, and in witnessing opportunities.

One of the prayer conference student leaders at Andrews University has been Rachel Johnson.

On the first weekend of May 1988, she led out at a prayer conference at a church at Grand Haven, Michigan. During the 11:00 o'clock hour Rachel called such conferences "miracle territory." This book focuses on how our personal lives can become miracle territory *now!*

"WE NEED MORE PRAYER!"

In God's providence Delinda Snyder brought the prayer and ministry conference idea to Andrews University when she enrolled in the fall of 1996 as a freshman. Much of the inspiration for the first book of this series, *30 Days to a More Powerful Prayer Life*, came from her burden to see more and more prayer, and from the many such conferences she has directed. Time and again she has exclaimed, "Pastor Joe, we need more prayer!"

Delinda had been one of seven students from Spring Valley Academy, in Dayton, Ohio, who in April of 1996 had gone to England as a part of a group of ninety teens who conducted prayer conferences in the South England Conference. Upon their return to Spring Valley, God used them to wonderfully change the spiritual atmosphere on that campus.

When Delinda came to Andrews, she came with a dream: regular prayer conferences on the Andrews campus. In God's providence she and another student, Philip Baptiste, led out in the first prayer conference put on by Andrews students—one at Broadview Academy in January of 1997 that led to decisions for baptism by several Broadview students. During the spring of 1997 she also led two conferences for adults—one at Worthington, Ohio, and another at the Wyoming Church in Grand Rapids, Michigan.

After two conferences during the fall of 1997, one at Bass Academy and another at Kingsway College, she saw her dream fulfilled—a conference at Andrews during the winter quarter and another during the spring quarter of the 1997–98 school year. God used both to deepen spiritual life on the Andrews campus.

I have now attended a dozen prayer conferences—sometimes as an observer, and other times as one of the organizing sponsors—since going to my first at Dakota Academy in June of 1996. Each has taken participants into "miracle territory"—with conversions and re-conversions that affect eternity itself.

PRAYER AS MIRACLE TERRITORY

Prayer itself, if backed by faith in the blood of Christ, puts one into miracle territory. Let me illustrate with a miracle that just took place. My computer is a Word Perfect purchased in 1991. Its hard drive is so full that on a Monday in early June I decided to make room for more content by deleting some files.

Everything that relates to my Workshop in Prayer class I file under WP. I started deleting WPs and got into the parent file, where Word Perfect directories are also listed as WP. I deleted so many of the directories that I lost access to everything. An individual who knows computers worked more than an hour but simply couldn't get access to the files. It looked like I might have lost the entire library.

I called a second consultant. He, too, tried everything he knew. As I sat and watched, you can believe that I did a lot of praying, but he finally said, "I just can't recover anything."

He then said, "Let me try one more thing." He did, and within less than a minute God helped him recover everything, including the manuscript for this book!

Now, every time I sit down at the computer, I praise God for that miracle. In humility and gratitude, I realize that I am entering *miracle territory.*

Shortly afterwards, something else happened that has made every time I sit down at my computer seem like an entry into miracle territory. My wife had decided to change the compost pile at the base of a back-yard cherry tree into a flower bed, and asked me to cut some limbs into short lengths to be used as boundary.

Just as I was cutting the last pieces, the chain saw slipped and cut into three fingers of my left hand. Had that taken off those fingers, this book might never have been completed. Through God's mercy, as I sit down at the computer, I do so with healing scars to remind me that I am entering miracle territory.

USABLE IDEAS

With new understandings we "use them or lose them." Consider these options:

- *Ask God to give you a two-fold passion: a passion for lost people, and a passion for prayer.*
- *Discuss this chapter with a family member or friend, asking questions like: What are the characteristics of prayer without passion? What changes might a passion for prayer bring into one's spiritual experience?*
- *If you have a copy of* 30 Days to a More Powerful Prayer Life, *see the chapter titled "A Spirit of Intercession" for more information about prayer and ministry conferences.*

Chapter 2

100,000 Spirit-Filled Youth

"The eyes of the Lord run to and fro throughout the whole earth,
to show Himself strong on behalf of those
whose heart is loyal to Him."
(2 Chronicles 16:9)

A full-of-energy little guy named Tim had developed the habit of reading something from the Gospels each day. One evening, when his mother was upstairs caring for the younger children, she noticed he was unusually quiet. Thinking he might be up to mischief, she asked, "Tim, what are you doing?"

"I'm watching Jesus raise Lazarus from the dead," he replied.

I had a similar experience one extremely cold Friday evening in March of 1998, except that I was watching Jesus die on the cross. It happened like this:

During the latter part of January, and through all of February 1988, southwest Michigan set a new record: no snow for nearly six weeks. Then in March a blizzard roared in on the second Tuesday and shut down everything.

The bitter cold remained through the weekend. On Friday evening my wife had gone to the hospital to be with a family member. I decided to skip everything on campus, light a fire in the fireplace, and spend the evening at Calvary.

I turned to Matthew 27 and tried to visualize the scenes pictured there: the scourging of Christ, the crown of thorns slammed onto His head, the actual crucifixion. I asked questions like, "What is there to see? To hear? To feel?"

After Christ had been nailed to the cross, the record says of the soldiers: "And sitting down they watched him there" (Matthew 27:36, KJV). I pictured my wife and myself as also watching, except we were kneeling at the foot of the cross.

SEEKING A FULL SURRENDER

Earlier I had almost memorized this definition of surrender to Christ:

> Surrender means the uttermost giving up of all we have and are to the mastery of Jesus—our worst, our best, our possessions, our past, our future, our life plans, our loved ones, our will, our *self.* That is surrender (A. G. Daniells, *A Leader of Men,* page 91).

I sought that kind of surrender, especially the total submission of self. With it I needed something closely related—grace to live up to all I know. For several days, in fact, God had impressed me with this statement of Jesus: "Man shall not live by bread alone, but by every word that proceeds from the mouth of God" (Matthew 4:4). I had also come across this comment:

> Not by one word, not by many words, but by every word that God has spoken, man shall live. We cannot disregard one word, however trifling it may seem to us, and be safe (*Thoughts From the Mount of Blessing,* page 52).

Thus on that Friday evening I wanted to renew a total surrender to Christ, with a commitment to live by every word God has given. There at the foot of the cross, in my imagination my wife and I looked up, and with broken hearts we watched as Christ's blood fell drop by drop to the rocks below. "It's for us!" we whispered.

As we renewed the kind of surrender described, in my imagination a prayer conference leader came to join us, and then other students we knew. Youth kept coming until there was an army of 100,000 of them, from everywhere, pressing as close as they could get—all yielded in total surrender before the cross. That army—an army on its knees—stretched back as far as we could see.

Then denominational leaders, pastors, and thousands of laymen began to come. Soon a second 100,000 people were kneeling as close as possible to the cross.

BACK TO REALITY

That evening, and almost continually ever since, I have asked God to raise up, from all over the world, 100,000 Spirit-filled teens and young adults by the year 2001. I'm pleading for 50,000 young women like some I know on this campus, and 50,000 committed young men. I do the same in praying for 100,000 non-students—pleading that God will use them to help bring the "revival of primitive godliness" that the Seventh-day Adventist Church must have in order to receive the latter rain.

"The eyes of the Lord," the bold print at the start of this chapter states, "run to and fro throughout the whole earth, to show Himself strong in behalf of those whose heart is loyal to Him" (2 Chronicles 16:9). He is looking for an army—youth, leaders, laymen, all "rightly trained"—that He can use to help usher in the return of Christ (*Education* 271).

In my praying I generally mention specific young men that I know and love by name—Philip, Eric, Jonathan, William, Greg, Dan, and others—and plead with intensity for them. In so doing I word my prayers to include *all* the 50,000 I am asking God to raise up and fill with His Spirit. I do the same for the 50,000 young women—Larra, Deanna, Antigoni, Priscilla, Tehani, Delinda, and others—always mentioning that I am asking God to raise up 50,000 others like them.

I believe that God literally is searching the earth for youth and older folk whom He can *totally possess,* and then through them begin the latter rain. It may not take 100,000 youth and another 100,000 adults, for God does not depend on numbers; in Gideons's time He used 300 rather than 30,000 men to get a task done. He simply couldn't use people who lacked humility and commitment.

The reason I ask for a total of 200,000 totally surrendered and dedicated people as we enter the next century is twofold:

- Every person who becomes a fully-surrendered "laborer together with God" (1 Corinthians 3:9, KJV) experiences the greatest of all earthly joys—seeing God work powerfully in their own lives and seeing people won to Christ. I want *as many as possible* to experience that kind of joy.
- 100,000 Spirit-filled youth working with 100,000 non-youth leaders and laymen, through a large outpouring of the Holy Spirit, could bring millions to the foot of the cross. In closing my prayer, in fact, I almost always ask for special blessings for the tens of millions that during earth's final hours God will bring to Himself.

PROMISES OF LATTER RAIN BLESSINGS

In Palestine there are two rainy seasons. During Bible times an early rain at planting time sprouted the seed and gave the crops a good start. A latter rain at harvest time filled out the grain.

In his Acts 2 sermon Peter referred to the outpouring of the Holy Spirit on the day of Pentecost as a fulfillment of Joel's prophecy (Acts 2:16-21, see Joel 2:28-32). That sermon led to the baptism of 3,000 people. Acts 2 ends with this summary statement about the growth that followed: "And the Lord added to the church daily such as should be saved" (Acts 2:47, KJV). Within the first twelve months after Pentecost, in fact, some 20,000 new members were added to the Jerusalem congregation (see Acts 2:41, 4:4, 5:14, 6:7).

The deep moving of the Holy Spirit at that time has been called "the early rain." These showers helped give the gospel a good start.

The "latter rain" can be expected just before Jesus returns. The following prophecy will again be fulfilled with even greater power:

> And it shall come to pass afterward That I will pour out My Spirit on all flesh. Your sons and your daughters shall prophesy. Your old men shall dream dreams, Your young men shall see visions. And also on My menservants and on My maidservants, I will pour out My Spirit in those days (Joel 2:28, 29).

In the context Joel mentions signs of the last days: blood, fire, and columns of smoke. He then gives this gracious promise: "And it shall come to pass that all who call upon the name of the Lord shall be delivered" (Joel 2:32, RSV).

At that time conversions will take place with a rapidity similar to what happened in the opening chapters of Acts. Thousands, even millions, will accept the gospel. Many of these new believers will almost immediately go to work sharing what they have discovered.

PEOPLE ON THEIR KNEES

The launching of the gospel started with a group of people on their knees. "They all joined together constantly in prayer" (Acts 1:14, NIV)—but they did more than pray. In a chapter entitled "Pentecost" the author of *The Acts of the Apostles* sums up what else they did:

- Engaged in deep searching of hearts
- Humbled their hearts in true repentance
- Confessed their unbelief
- Put away their differences and drew close together in Christian fellowship
- Drew nearer and still nearer to God
- Developed an earnest desire to see lost people brought to Christ

Note the last development listed. As their love for Christ grew *they started really caring for people.* They wanted to get out and make a difference! For this they sought the energy and power available through the Holy Spirit.

The following suggestion was given about 1895:

The descent of the Holy Spirit upon the church is looked forward to as in the future; but it is the privilege of the church to have it now. Seek for it, pray for it, believe for it. We must have it, and Heaven is waiting to bestow it (*Evangelism*, page 701).

Seek for it, pray for it, believe for it

The church needs Spirit-filled leaders who will seek and pray and believe. It needs youth and young adults who will seek and pray and believe. It needs millions of all ages who will develop a spirit of supplication.

If not now, when? If not you, who? If not at your church, or at your campus, or in your home, where?

USABLE IDEAS

As you think about the ideas in this chapter, you might want to consider doing one or more of the following:

- *Evaluate the definition of surrender given in this chapter and compare it with your own experience at the present time. Ask, "Have I made this kind of surrender to Jesus?"*

- *Prayerfully study Christ's statement in Matthew 4:4 about living by "every word" God has spoken. Search your heart, asking, "What duties given in God's Word am I ignoring?" For two samples that have to do with family life, see Ephesians 4:32 and 5:1-4.*

- *The author of* The Desire of Ages *suggests that in the study of the life of Christ we "should take it point by point, and let the imagination grasp each scene, especially the closing ones" (page 83). For a several-day devotional experience, read a few paragraphs a day from the chapter in* The Desire of Ages *entitled "Calvary." Ask questions such as, "What is there to see? To hear? To feel?"*

Chapter 3

Dwight Nelson: "Meet My Savior— an Eyewitness Account"

"God has shown how much he loves us—
it was while we were still sinners that Christ died for us. . . .
We were God's enemies, but he made us
his friends through the death of his Son."
(Romans 5:6-10, TEV)

Dwight Nelson, who became senior pastor at the Pioneer Memorial Church on the campus of Andrews University in May of 1983, gave the following testimony at the start of the 1983–84 school year. I share it here with his permission.

The dictionary definition of the word is short and simple—Savior: one that saves, delivers, or preserves from danger or destruction. Today I would like to invite you to meet my Savior. It just so happens that I have two of them, a little "s" savior— in a few moments he will come from over there. The big "S" Savior—want you to meet Him too. Someday [pointing up] He'll come from there.

One savior you will see this morning with your eyes. But O how I am praying that you will see the other Savior with your heart. I want you to meet both of them, for I met them seven and eight years ago at a school called Andrews University. And while you will be hearing a story about me, please know that I am sharing it as a story about them.

It happened in the summer of '55. I was three and three-tenths years years of age. I was born with three words stamped on my spine, "Made in Japan." I spent fourteen years of my life in Japan, where my parents were missionaries. We were at a mountain lake, Nojirii, tucked away in the mountains of central Japan—a quiet lake that during summer vacation brought missionaries from all over Japan.

It was a Sunday evening. A large group of Adventist missionaries gathered on a hillside that sloped down to the lake.

Men were stoking a blazing fire, getting ready for a corn roast, laughing and sharing together. Wives were in their little groups. Kids were racing up and down the grassy hill. Fog was slipping down to meet the steamy warmth of the lake.

It was not a good time for swimming. The shadows were too are dark, and besides there was a corn roast coming, and so I and all the children were sternly warned not to go near the lonely dock. Mother was off with my six-month-old baby brother. Dad was with the other husbands.

I was supposed to be with the other kids, but my little feet were making their way to forbidden ground. The fog was creeping up onto the dock. Nobody would see me, nobody would know.

I don't recall what happened. Perhaps I was trying to throw a stone or leaning over to see the clear lake bottom. All I know is that there was a muffled splash, and I who could not swim or scream went under, in waters too deep for survival. No one knew, no one saw. Another three-year-old was drowning all alone.

MY LITTLE "S" SAVIORS

Those were the schemes of the prince of darkness, but I believe that another kingdom had another a dream.

An Adventist military couple, a chaplain, had come to be with other Adventists for the weekend. One of the missionaries had offered a boat excursion around the lake. Then without warning, as the fog began to settle down, the boat driver said, "We must go in now." He went to the dock and tied up the boat, and the military couple walked up to the shore.

Both saw it at the same instant. Off to their right, in the deep water, lying face down and motionless, the body of a three-year-old. The woman screamed, the husband jumped into the water, and the wife, who could not swim, jumped in behind her husband. Oh I wish I could recall that moment when my little face was lifted from of the waters of death and I gazed into the face of my savior.

For many years I never knew their names. I'm sure my parents mentioned them over and over again, to drive home the lesson of obedience, and to impress upon my young heart that there was a divine destiny for my life. But I was young, and the names didn't make a lasting impression. So I grew up with the story of being saved, but I never knew my little "s" savior, nor my big "S" Savior.

BORN SAVED

I was "born saved," and grew up in a home where Jesus was sung about in morning and evening worships. I attended Seventh-day Adventist schools from grade one to graduate schools—good schools where you get graded on how well you know the facts about Jesus. That was the problem. You know the facts yet know nothing about a friendship with Jesus.

It was not the fault of my parents, it was not the fault of my teachers. They tried to get the message to me, but always I fell back on that assurance that I was born saved. So when weeks of prayer came, and invitations were given to come forward, I didn't need to. I had never fallen away. There was no reason why God could not save this fifth-generation Adventist.

I graduated from Southern Missionary College in 1973, to become a fourth-generation Seventh-day Adventist minister. I interned in Oregon as a youth pastor for a year, and it was great. I fell more deeply in love with a Southern blossom I had met at college, we were married in June of 1974, and what a life! Married, happy, secure. I needed nothing, I needed no one.

That September we arrived at Andrews University. I registered. I took the first quarter's classes. Cocky and proud, confident and brash, I had it all—good grades, good friends, and great racquetball. What more could I want?

Christmas break—I was praying before going to bed, as a born-saved young man should. But there on my knees I sensed something was missing. I couldn't put my finger on it, but I felt like the rich young ruler: I had everything—but something was missing.

FINDING WHAT WAS MISSING

And then as I was on my knees the words of a professor from the previous quarter came back to me. He had been speaking to us from Psalm 19 and said,

"Gentlemen, we should ask God to reveal our hidden sins, our true nature."

I thought, "That's it, I'll pray that prayer. I don't have a lot to confess. It won't take God very long. I'll get it out of the way." I did, felt better, and went to bed.

Later I learned from my favorite author that when you pray that prayer, you better quickly pray, "God, show me a sin-pardoning Savior."

But I didn't know that other half, I hadn't met Him, you see. I crawled into bed, not knowing I was destined for darkness.

A few weeks later we were coming back from Christmas vacation in North Carolina. I can still remember that moment. We were just crossing the Kentucky-Indiana border when a dark, heavy cloud fell over me. I changed the radio dial, thinking maybe it was the music, but the darkness didn't go away.

We came back to this campus, New Year's Eve was the next day, and as I struggled with the darkness I thought maybe it was because I hadn't made my New Year's resolutions. So I wrote out my resolutions. But that cloud didn't go away; it got blacker.

I thought maybe I wasn't exercising enough, so I started that, but it didn't work either. I started lying awake at night, staring up at the ceiling. I would break out into a cold sweat, and suddenly I thought, "Maybe there is no God, no heaven."

I was scared to tell my wife, afraid she wouldn't understand. I desperately needed to talk to someone, and then it started happening, little matters out of the past, sins I had forgotten. They were all there, and all I could see was a black pit. I was hopeless and I was helpless. I had to talk to someone. But I didn't know to whom I could turn. And then I thought of that professor. After all, it was his idea.

So I found him after class, and in a faltering manner I poured out scant details of my agony, afraid I was going to burst into tears. I was hoping he'd put his arm about me and take me into his office where I could talk. I don't think he intended to be gruff, but he said, "Go read *Steps to Christ*."

I'm bleeding, I need to talk, and he tells me to go read a book! Hurt, confused, and desperate, I went home, pulled down that little paperback, and thumbed through. I read:

It is impossible for us of ourselves to escape from that pit of sin into which we are sunken. . . . There must be a power working from within, a new life from above. That power is Christ. His grace alone can quicken the lifeless faculties of the soul, and attract it to God (page 18).

On I read, and I came to these words:

> As you see the enormity of sin, as you see yourself as you really are, do not give up in despair. It was sinners that Christ came to save. We have not to reconcile God to us, but—O wondrous love!—God in Christ is 'reconciling the world unto Himself.' 2 Corinthians 5:19. He is wooing by His tender love the hearts of His erring children (page 35).

FINDING MY BIG "S" SAVIOR

Lost and alone, I remember looking out the window, to the gray, blustery winter clouds, and I tell you, it was as if I could see the face of the Father, and He had on His face a tender, compassionate look. He was looking at me, and I remember crying out, choked with emotion, and dim with tears. "God, if you will, I want to come home, I've got to be saved."

And *Steps to Christ* became a self-fulfilling prophecy. You see, I met Jesus. He had always been there, for my proud, self-sufficient life. But this time I met Him when I needed Him. I desperately needed His friendship, I could not live without His friendship. I begged Him, Can I have You? And He said Yes. I who had nothing to offer except the shame of my own guilt, met Him who has everything to offer. I met Jesus.

Every early morning now I go to meet Him, not because I am trying to earn a place somewhere up in His heaven. I go to meet Him because I need some quiet time with my Friend. As long as there is breath in me, I will cling to this friendship.

Do you understand? Gone the guilt, gone the fear, gone the cloud, gone the frustration of trying to make it on my own. Now there was peace, now there was power and the promise of eternity with this Friend. And you know what? I sleep like a baby now.

And I want you to meet my Savior. Because He's my friend now. I want you to meet both of them, my little "s" savior, and my big "S" Savior.

Space does not permit any more first person relation of how the message ended. Pastor Dwight told us that about a year after his conversion, at a meeting of some shirt-tail relatives, the military couple previously mentioned was also present. As the couple, chaplain and Mrs. Glenn Bowen, visited with Pastor Dwight, they discovered he was the three-year-old they had pulled from the lake.

To close the service that Sabbath morning, Pastor Dwight introduced the Bowens to his congregations at both services. "Little did they know," he said, "that twenty-eight years ago they were pulling their senior pastor out of the water. And now we serve together. My little 's' savior and I on the same staff, serving our big 'S' Savior."

MAKING IT PERSONAL

Do you find anything in this story that fits your situation? Here are some options to consider:

- *If you already have chosen Christ as your Savior,* Steps to Christ *suggests, "Consecrate yourself to God in the morning; make this your very first work. Let your prayer be, 'Take me, O Lord, as wholly Thine. I lay all my plans at Thy feet. Use me today in Thy service. Abide with me, and let all my work be wrought in Thee.' "*
- *If the above doesn't describe your present experience, you might want to think of becoming a Christian as a transaction. You choose to tell Christ, "Lord Jesus, I need You. I am a sinner, and I need Your forgiveness. I choose to turn away from all known sin. Please cleanse me and give me a new heart. Thank You for accepting me. In Your name I pray. Amen."*
- *The book* Steps to Christ *contains a chapter titled "Faith and Acceptance" that you may find helpful. After making a decision for Christ, many people need this assurance: "Do not wait to feel that you are made whole, but say, 'I believe it; it is so, not because I feel it, but because God has promised' "* (Steps to Christ, *page 5).*

Chapter 4

A Passion for Perspective

"I counsel you to . . . anoint your eyes with eye salve,
that you may see."
(Revelation 3:18)

In *Power to Change Your Life* Rick Warren quotes a letter that a collegian had written to her parents:

Dear Mom and Dad:

I'm sorry to be so long in writing. Unfortunately, all my stationery was destroyed the night our dorm was set on fire by the demonstrators. I'm out of the hospital now and the doctors say my eyesight should return—sooner or later. The wonderful boy, Bill, who rescued me from the fire, kindly offered to share his little apartment with me until the dorm is rebuilt. He comes from a good family, so you won't be surprised when I tell you we're going to be married. In fact, since you've always wanted a grandchild, you'll be glad to know that you'll be grandparents next month.

P.S. Please disregard the above practice in English composition. There was no fire, I haven't been in the hospital, I'm not pregnant, and I don't even have a steady boyfriend. But I did get a D in French and an F in Chemistry, and I just wanted to be sure you received this news in the proper perspective.

Perspective has to do with the relationship of parts to the whole, the ability to see the whole picture. It helps one get a sharp, clear grasp of issues.

Christ did it lovingly, but in His attempts to get people to look at things clearly, He often asked questions. In *Jesus the Revolutionary* H. S. Vigeveno includes a chapter titled "The Questioning Jesus." In it he says: "Someone has gone to the arduous task of adding up these questions, and has found two hundred and thirteen of them asked by Jesus in the gospels" (page 86).

There is some duplication, of course. Through questions Jesus sought to make people think, to look clearly at life and death issues. "The questions of Jesus are sharp as an arrow, aimed with precision," Vigeveno says. "They strike their mark. And their overall purpose is for decision!" (page 87).

AN EXAMPLE

What does study of Christ's questions reveal? "First," Vigeveno wrote, "we see Jesus cutting through the jungle of muddled thinking. He aims at our minds! Our minds must be changed, for only he who is convinced will commit himself. We must be persuaded before we decide. So Jesus marshals His facts, states His case, asks His questions, aims at our intellect" (Ibid.).

In Mark 8:34-38 He prepares His listener's minds for the questions He intends to ask by saying: "Whoever desires to come after Me, let him deny himself, and take up his cross, and follow Me. For whoever desires to save his life will lose it, but whoever loses his life for My sake and the gospel's will save it."

Jesus then asks: "For what will it profit a man if he gains the whole world, and loses his own soul? Or what will a man give in exchange for his soul?"

He concludes with this powerful appeal: "For whoever is ashamed of Me and My words in this adulterous and sinful generation, of him the Son of Man also will be ashamed when He comes in the glory of His Father with the holy angels."

You can't fail to get His point!

FROM THE JERUSALEM POST

Jesus also used current events in an attempt to get people to think. Take, for example, the headline in the Jerusalem Post about the Galileans whose blood Pilate had mingled with sacrifices. And, also, the front-page story about eighteen citizens who had been killed when a tower in Siloam had fallen (Luke 13:1-5). Jesus turned both news items into a double appeal for repentance. First He asked: "Do you suppose these Galileans were worse sinners than all other Galileans?"

He then said: "I tell you no, but unless you repent you will all likewise perish" (verse 3).

Jesus continued, "Or those eighteen on whom the tower in Siloam fell and killed them, do you think they were worse sinners than all the other men who dwelt in Jerusalem?" As a second punch line He said, "I tell you no, but unless you repent you will all likewise perish."

Vigeveno sums up Christ's method: "He aims at the mind, arouses the conscience, appeals to the emotions, and finally assails the will. Here we make our choice. And reach a verdict we must. When intellectually convinced, conscientiously aroused, emotionally involved, we must choose" (page 94).

GIVING IT STRAIGHT

"Is it lawful for a man to divorce his wife?" the Pharisees once asked Christ. Jesus told them that the divorce concessions God had allowed in the Old Testament were because of the hardhearted ways of His people (Mark 10:2, 4, 5; see Deuteronomy 24:1-4).

Later the disciples brought the subject up again. Peterson's The Message paraphrase introduces Christ's reply like this, "Jesus gave it to them straight." He said, "A man who divorces his wife so he can marry someone else commits adultery against her. And a woman who divorces her husband so she can marry someone else commits adultery" (Mark 10:10-12).

Jesus gave it to them straight.

Here, again, is what God is up to: "The eyes of the Lord run to and fro throughout the whole earth, to show Himself strong on behalf of those whose heart is loyal to Him" (2 Chronicles 16:9).

What kind of person—young or otherwise—is God looking for? Isaiah answers: "On this one will I look: on him who is poor and of a contrite spirit, and who trembles at My word" (Isaiah 66:2). Three requirements: Humility. Into the Word. Obedience to the Word. In other words, humble people seeking by God's grace to live "by every word that proceeds out of the mouth of God" (Matthew 4:4).

Here almost all of us tend to come short. Instead of trembling at unwelcome truths, we make excuses, rationalize, attempt to explain away.

In John 10 Christ presented Himself as the good Shepherd, and declared, "I am come that they might have life, and that they might have it more abundantly" (John 10:10). Does the "every word" requirement contradict that?

Not really. Love turns obedience into delight. A book I have sometimes used to encourage students to do daily devotional reading, *My Life Today*, has a page with comments on Proverbs 23:26—a text that invites us to give our hearts to God and then *keep* His ways. The author's comments include this insight:

> Those who feel the constraining love of God do not ask how little may be given to meet the requirements of God; they do not ask for the lowest standard, but aim at perfect conformity to the will of their Redeemer. With earnest desire they yield all, and manifest an interest proportionate to the value of the object which they seek (page 7).

And what's "the object which they seek"? Eternal life! Life that will never, never end! To ever explore new thoughts! To ever find new wonders! To ever increase in capacity to know, to love, to enjoy! To know that beyond will ever be more and more and still more of everything that thrills and delights!

And not just for yourself, but for all you can influence to choose Jesus and life.

TRUTHS THAT TRANSFORM

What will transform us into the godly, loyal, fully committed people that the eyes of the Lord are scanning the earth to find? I see four sources for the power we need:

The cross and the blood shed there

When Paul wrote to the people in Colossae, at least some in that congregation needed victory over things like "fornication, uncleanness, passion, evil desire, and covetousness," along with "anger, wrath, malice, blasphemy, filthy language" (Colossians 3:5, 8).

In a prayer recorded in Colossians 1:9-14 Paul asked God to give them a "knowledge of His will in all wisdom and spiritual understanding," that they might have "a walk worthy of the Lord, fully pleasing Him, being fruitful in every good work and increasing in the knowledge of God." He concludes his prayer with a focus on the blood of Christ: "In whom we have redemption through His blood, the forgiveness of sins."

The Word of God

In Hebrews 4, Paul describes that Word as "living and powerful, and sharper than any two-edged sword" (verse 12). He then directs us to Christ as our "great High Priest" who was "in all points tempted as we are, yet without sin." He's there to defend us against Satan's accusations. "Let us therefore," Paul urges, "come boldly to the throne of grace, that we may obtain mercy, and find grace to help in time of need" (verses 15, 16).

The life changes that take place through the Word are incredible. "The heart that receives the word of God . . . is like the mountain stream fed by unfailing springs, whose cool, sparkling waters leap from rock to rock, refreshing the weary, the thirsty, the heavy laden" (*Christ's Object Lessons*, 130).

The Holy Spirit

In Romans 7 Paul tells of his own struggles in seeking to live a godly life. He finds himself doing things he knows he shouldn't and exclaims, "O wretched man that I am! Who shall deliver me from this body of death?" He answers, "I thank God—through Jesus Christ" (verses 24, 25).

Then in Romans 8 Paul directs attention to the help that can be ours through the Holy Spirit, and tells us that "the Spirit Himself makes intercession for us with groanings which cannot be uttered" (verse 26).

The power of prayer

"Pray in the Spirit on all occasions with all kinds of prayers and requests," Paul urges. "Be always alert and keep on praying . . . Pray . . . Pray" (Ephesians 6:18-20, NIV).

It's through prayer that we appropriate the blood of Christ. It's through prayer that we lay hold of the promises in God's Word. It's as we pray that the Holy Spirit flows into our lives. Let's pray, pray, pray, pray.

In his book *Mighty Prevailing Prayer* Wesley Duewel asks, "Do you want to see the tide of battle turned and Christ proved victor in battle after battle on earth today?" He suggests, "Get the church to prevailing. Enlist and train the believers in prayer warfare. . . . No battle is too nearly lost for God to win. No combination of opposing forces is too strong or too numerous for God. Forward on your knees!" (page 236).

Duewel then pleads:

> Stand in the victory of Calvary. Glory in the defeat of Satan at Calvary. Insist on enforcing the victory of Calvary. Enter into mighty prayer warfare, with the name of Jesus, the infallible Word of God, and the blood of Calvary your confidence and your invincible weapons (Ibid.).

The Cross and the blood. The Word of God. The Holy Spirit. The power available through prayer. May God give us the good sense, the perspective that will lead us to depend more and still more on all four of these life-changing resources!

SELECTING USABLE IDEAS

The Laodicean message, in Revelation 3:14-22, describes some of the problems in the last generation of believers. In the text that starts this chapter, eye salve is suggested as a remedy for perception problems. Here are some questions and exercises related to discernment.

- *For a study of questions that Jesus asked to get people to think, and bring them to conviction, spend a little time, alone or in a small group, with the question or questions in Matthew 16:13-17 or John 5:44-47.*
- *Does seeking to live "by every word" seem rigid? Did Adam and Eve think so when they ate one piece of forbidden fruit?*
- *For discussion: It has been said that when Jesus corrected people, He had "tears in His voice." Can a parent correct a child or teenager that way? If so, how?*

Chapter 5

Brokenness at the Cross

"Whoever falls on this stone will be broken;
but on whomever it falls,
it will grind him to powder."
(Matthew 21:44)

At a prayer conference in late May 1998, we had been studying the passage in Matthew 21 that includes the preceding statement of Jesus. As the study neared its close, a young mother started crying. "I feel like I'm falling on the Rock," she said, "and I'm putting out my hands as I fall."

Earlier that day Philip Baptiste, an Andrews University student who was leading the conference, had given a message which he titled "Saved by Grace, Spared by Mercy." Philip, a business and religion major, had preached with so much of the Holy Spirit's power that all of us had been deeply moved. That afternoon the two dozen adults at the conference had gathered for a group Bible study and were discussing the closing verses of Matthew 21. We had seated ourselves in a circle, with Philip the facilitator. We used the AAA method—*Ask, Answer,* and *Apply.*

To introduce it Philip asked, "Do you use a juicer? A juicer takes carrots or fruit, and extracts the best part—that with vitamins and nutrients. That's what the AAA method of Bible study does: it takes a passage and juices it."

"We first read a short passage," he explained. "Then we go around the circle, and take turns reading and exploring one verse at a time. We try to ask all kinds of questions: Who? When? Why? Where? What? We then use the context, cross references, or other passages as we look for answers.

"To conclude the study, we "juice out" ideas we can use. We want things we can apply to our daily lives."

It was as applications were being juiced that a young woman started crying. I had gotten acquainted with her earlier in the day. About a year earlier, she said, she had been visiting various churches in Grand Rapids, Michigan to find one that taught the Bible. She hadn't found one she liked, but then she met a young couple from the Bethel Seventh-day Adventist Church in that city. They had built a friendship with her, and she became a regular attender at their church. They had brought her to the prayer conference at the Miracle Meadows camp near Kalamazoo, Michigan.

As tears trickled, Philip suggested, "Let's all gather around this young woman, pray, and lay hands on her." Tears came for more than one during that time of prayer. Then a little later, as we closed the session by praying in teams of two, I prayed with a young man on my right. He, too, had been moved by the Bible study and mentioned he had come to Christ just a year earlier.

A PARABLE ABOUT VINEDRESSERS

The context for the passage we studied is this: the priests and elders had confronted Jesus, and He had spoken the parable of the wicked vinedressers (Matthew 21:33-40). At harvest time the owner of a vineyard sent servants to get produce. The vinedressers had "beat one, killed one, and stoned another."

"Again he sent other servants . . . and they did likewise to them. Then last of all he sent his son to them saying, 'They will respect my son' " (verses 35-37). But they had murdered the son, and Jesus asked, "Therefore when the owner of the vineyard comes, what will he do to those vinedressers?" (verse 40).

At first the elders and priests didn't realize that the parable was about them. "He will destroy those wicked men miserably," they replied, "and lease his vine-

yard to other vinedressers who will render to him the fruits in their seasons"
(verse 41).

Jesus then quoted this prophecy from the Psalms: "The stone which the
builders rejected has become the chief cornerstone" (Psalm 118:22). He ended
His parable by saying:

> Therefore I say to you, the kingdom will be taken from you, and given to
> a nation bearing the fruits of it. And whoever falls on the stone will be broken;
> but on whomever it falls, it will grind him to powder (pages 43, 44).

PAINFUL CHOICES

During our discussion we noted that both alternatives are painful. We can
come to Christ, and be broken in repentance for our sins, or reject Him and be
ground to powder. *The Desires of Ages* gives this interpretation: "To fall upon the
Rock and be broken is to give up our self-righteousness and go to Christ with
the humility of a child, repenting of our transgressions and believing in His
forgiving love" (page 599).

Notice the steps I need to take to be broken:

- Give up my self-righteousness
- Go to Christ like a child
- Repent of my sins
- Believe He forgives me

That's what I want! I want to be totally broken every day at the foot of the
cross. More and more and still more!

In chapter 2 I told my dream: 100,000 Spirit-filled youth kneeling as close
to the cross as they can get. Then with them 100,000 leaders and laymen also
pressing in to kneel in total surrender to Christ, with both groups committed to
"live by every word that proceeds out of the mouth of God" (Matthew 4:4).

The above steps are simple and easy to understand. Will you join me at the foot
of the cross? Can we experience the joys of brokenness together?

APPLICATIONS

The Miracle Meadows Camp, which the Bethel church rented from the
Evangelical Mennonite owners, proved to be just that—Miracle Meadows. There

is no miracle that equals the miracle of being broken at the foot of the cross.

In John 5 Jesus compared the miracle of conversion to the miracle of a resurrection from the dead: "Most assuredly," He had said, "I say to you, the hour is coming, and now is, when the dead will hear the voice of the Son of God, and those who hear will live" (John 5:25).

When Jesus said this, He had not yet raised anyone from physical death. When I compare His statement with the opening verses of Ephesians 2, where Paul talks about being dead in trespasses and sin, I conclude that Jesus was talking about being raised from spiritual death. As I prepared a syllabus for my Workshop in Prayer class, I discovered this: "To arouse those spiritually dead, to create new tastes, new motives, requires as great an outlay of power as to raise one from physical death" (Ellen White in *Review and Herald,* 12 March 1901).

Astonishing! Amazing! When God uses you to help someone come and kneel at the foot of the cross in brokenness and surrender, that's a miracle just as surely as if you were to lay hands on a corpse and bring it back to life!

As you think about the truths in this chapter, here are possible applications and enrichments:

- *Evaluate and pray about the four steps that lead to brokenness, as given in this chapter. Compare your own experience with them.*
- *Brokenness at the cross and repentance are closely related. In personal study or in a small group, why not spend some time with the chapter in* Steps to Christ *titled "Repentance"?*
- *The AAA method of Bible study can be used with as few as two or three people. You might want to get together with two or more and give it a try. One option: Ephesians 2:1-7. Another: Matthew 21:42-44.*

Chapter 6

A Passion to Hate Sin

"I will put enmity between you and the woman,
And between your seed and her Seed:
He shall bruise your head,
And you shall bruise His heel."
(Genesis 3:15)

Before starting meetings in a large city an evangelist wrote a letter to the mayor. In it he asked for names of people the mayor knew who had spiritual problems, and needed prayer. The mayor sent a copy of the entire city directory.

Romans 3:23—"All have sinned and fall short"—takes in all of us. All need the two things the above promise offers: a Savior, and a hatred for sin.

Genesis 3:15 is the first promise in the Bible, and the first one we underline in our Workshop in Prayer class. I generally tell students: "In Genesis 3:15 God is talking to Lucifer, but the promise is for us. The Seed is Jesus our Savior, and with a Savior God also promises to help us to hate sin." As a comment I give students this statement from *The Great Controversy:* "God declares, 'I will put enmity.' This enmity is not naturally entertained. . . . It is the grace that Christ implants in the soul which creates in man enmity against Satan" (pages 505, 506).

Against that background, let's take a look at some Bible facts about sin and grace, and conclude with some suggestions about how to develop a hatred for sin.

FACTS ABOUT SIN

Sin is deadly

In Romans 6:23 Paul says so in six blunt words: "The wages of sin is death." That's the second death—a death that takes place in the lake of fire (Revelation 20:14). Paul quickly adds, however, "But the gift of God is eternal life" (Ibid.).

Sin is deceptive

If Satan were to get a tombstone, this phrase from Revelation 20:10 would be an appropriate epithet: "The devil, who deceived them." Or from John 8:44, this: "A liar, and the father of it."

Sin never brings lasting happiness

Jesus spoke of two ways: a narrow, upward way that "leads to life" and a broad way that "leads to destruction" (Matthew 7:13, 14). The entrance to the broad way promises much, but that way leads down, down, down. Solomon put it like this: "The way of transgressors is hard" (Proverbs 13:15, KJV).

No sin is small

Adam and Eve rationalized that taking a few bites from the forbidden fruit was inconsequential. It wasn't. And for us today: "Sin, however small it may be esteemed, can be indulged only at the peril of infinite loss. What we do not overcome will overcome us, and work out our destruction" (*Steps to Christ,* pages 32, 33).

No person—child, youth, adult—can be forced to sin

"God is faithful, who will not allow you to be tempted above what you are able, but with the temptation will also make the way of escape, that you may be able to bear it" (1 Corinthians 10:13).

A sin that we need to especially hate is pride

Pride led to Lucifer's rebellion (Ezekiel 28:17). As illustrated by the Pharisee and publican of Luke 18:9-13, pride and self-sufficiency are "the most hopeless, the most incurable" of all sins (*Christ's Object Lessons,* page 154).

God's Word shows an unforgiving spirit as another sin to especially hate
The Lord's Prayer contains six petitions; the only one Christ enlarged on was "Forgive us . . . as we forgive" (Matthew 6:9-14). Matthew 18 urges that we be willing to forgive offenses against us "seventy times seven" times (Matthew 18:22).

Through our dependence on the blood of Christ all sin can be overcome
"We have redemption through His blood, the forgiveness of sins" (Colossians 1:14). No matter how strong the temptation, urge the blood of Christ as you seek deliverance. "Satan . . . trembles and flees when the merits of that precious blood are urged" (*Testimonies for the Church,* vol. 5, page 317).

FACTS ABOUT GRACE

All along the upward way "the grace of God that brings salvation" (Titus 2:11) can be our constant support. Here are some facts about grace:

Grace is gracious
The dictionary defines *gracious,* from the root *grace,* as possessing or showing kindness, courtesy, charm, and also as merciful, compassionate. When, after the golden calf rebellion at Mt. Sinai, the Lord described Himself, He began, "The Lord, the Lord God, merciful and gracious . . . (Exodus 34:6).

Grace is generous
Romans 5, which is about victory over sin, mentions grace six times. Three of those six speak of the *abundance* of grace (see verses 15, 17, 20). Verse 20 says, "Where sin abounded, grace abounded much more."

Grace is gentle
Paul could be firm when necessary, but he was also gentle. In writing to the Thessalonians Paul declared, "We were gentle among you, just as a nursing mother cherishes her own children" (1 Thessalonians 2:7). And one of the fruits of the Spirit is gentleness (Galatians 5:22, 23).

Grace gives and gives and gives
Paul put it this way: "Our great God and Savior Jesus Christ . . . gave Himself for us, that He might redeem us from every lawless deed and purify for Himself His

own special people, zealous for good works" (Titus 2:13, 14).

Christ gave Himself! That's the absolute ultimate!

HATING SIN

The facts about sin given at the start of this chapter provide plenty of reason to hate it and shun it, but the awfulness of sin is best shown at Calvary. There Christ suffered every kind of pain that can be inflicted:

- The agony of being rejected by people you intensely love
- The anguish of being deserted by one's friends
- The torture that comes when one's back and abdomen have been shredded, and one's hands and feet have been pierced by spikes
- The choking awfulness of not being able to breathe except by trying to lift oneself by pressing on the feet, causing even more excruciating pain
- The horror of the darkness that came from being separated from the Father you intensely love

Crucifixion Friday is past for our precious Savior, but there is another pain that I—and you—keep inflicting on Him by what Paul calls "crucifying the Son of God all over again" (Hebrews 6:6, NIV). Consider this comment on the Beatitude about mourning:

By every sin Jesus is wounded afresh, and as we look upon Him whom we have pierced, we mourn for the sins which have brought anguish upon Him. Such mourning will lead to the renunciation of sin (*The Desire of Ages*, page 300).

I have made it a habit to mention the promise of Genesis 3:15 almost every morning, and at various times during the day. I do so, not just for myself, but in a collective way for Christian youth everywhere. As I focus on that promise, I like to picture myself kneeling at the foot of the cross. It becomes sharply vivid as I watch Christ's blood falling drop by drop onto the rocks at the foot of the cross.

FOUR THINGS GOD DOES NOT KNOW

In one of his messages given at the 1998 Wisconsin camp meeting, Morris Venden spoke about four things God does not know. Here are those four, with a summary statement about each:

1. God does not know a sin He does not hate.
God hates sin—all sin—because of what it does to people He loves.
2. God does not know a sinner He does not love.
God's great heart of love longs to reach every lost person. There is nothing a sinner can do that will cause God to stop loving him or her.
3. God does not know a sin He won't forgive.
There is an unpardonable sin, but that's the sin for which one does not ask pardon. The greater our sinfulness, the greater the Savior whom God provides.
4. God does not know a better time than now to choose Jesus as your Savior.
The Bible repeatedly emphasizes that *now* is the day of salvation.

PETTING A RATTLESNAKE

One July day in the North Carolina hills, three young boys went out to pick berries. They were to watch a nine-month-old baby brother, whom they left on some cool grass where he could be seen from where they were picking. After a time they heard the baby making "da, da, da" sounds. He seemed to be petting something.

Looking closer, they saw him petting a huge rattlesnake that lay across the baby's legs. Its face was close to the baby's face, who seemed totally unafraid.

What to do? The boys decided to do nothing, knowing that to disturb the snake would be fatal to the baby, who kept talking in soft tones and rubbing the sleek body of the snake. Finally the snake slithered away into the tall grass.

Sooner or later sin indulged becomes more deadly than rattlesnake venom. Let's ask God to give us such a hatred for deliberate sin that we will shun it like a rattlesnake!

SUGGESTIONS TO TEST

- *Try using Genesis 3:15 as you pray. I like to upon awakening. As you go through the day, you could ask again and again, "Father, according to Your promise, help me to hate sin."*
- *Which of the facts about grace do you most appreciate? Which ones need to be developed more fully in your life?*
- *Is there someone you know with whom you could share the four things God does not know? If so, see what reaction you get as you explain each one.*

Chapter 7

A Passion to Become Spirit-Filled

"Be filled with the Spirit."
(Ephesians 3:18)

One day Linda, who worked for me as a typist, opened up with her feelings about the Holy Spirit:

"During most of my academy years," she said, "I felt that the Holy Spirit was constantly watching me. His main task, I thought, was to make me feel guilty when I sinned. When a chapel speaker or minister talked about the Holy Spirit, I got uneasy. I especially disliked the idea of being 'filled' with the Spirit.

"What would happen if I were filled with the Holy Spirit, I wondered. Would He force me to do things I didn't want to do? And what did Jesus mean when He talked about the Holy Spirit convicting me of sin (John 16:8)? Is it His job to harass me when I do wrong?

"When I was a child adults told me, 'There are two voices that will speak to your heart. One belongs to Jesus; the other to Satan. When you are tempted, Jesus whispers, "Don't do it! Don't do it!" And Satan's voice says, "Aw, come on. Just once won't hurt. It would be a lot of fun.' "

"Later I found out that Jesus' voice was actually the Holy Spirit's voice. To me it seemed it was a voice that kept saying, 'Don't. Don't. Don't.' "

"By my junior year of academy I had begun to think of the Holy Spirit as constantly trying to make me feel lousy when I did wrong. The idea of being filled with such a Person frightened me."

Linda decided to do some research, and learned that the Holy Spirit was not like she thought. Here are some of the discoveries that changed her mind:

- The word *reprove* (used in he KJV's wording of John 16:8) can be translated as "convict" (NKJV) or "persuade" (RSV). To persuade people, she learned, does not mean to pressure them until they give in. To persuade means to help a person decide to do something by helping him to understand *why* he should do it.
- The Holy Spirit is symbolized by a dove (Matthew 3:16), the gentlest of birds. "One spring," Linda said, "I had a chance to watch a pair of doves teach a baby dove to fly, and I learned how affectionate and loving they are. I concluded that the Holy Spirit is the same way."
- In the King James Version the Holy Spirit is called "Comforter" (John 14:26). "I found out," Linda said, "that the word translated *Comforter* contains many ideas: Helper (TEV), Advocate (NEB), Counselor (NIV). But I especially liked Phillips' translation: Someone to 'stand by' you.

"FILLED WITH THE SPIRIT"

The April 13, 1998 issue of *Newsweek* contained an article titled "Living in the Holy Spirit." A caption read, " 'Spirit-led worship' is a body-shaking, soul stirring experience for millions of charismatic believers."

The authors included this description of a 2,000-person worship service in Pensacola, Florida: "As the huge congregation rises, the Spirit descends. Off comes shoes; this is holy ground. Young and old, black and brown and white alike, hop, twist, and dance in the aisles."

The article goes on to describe "a string of 'ooohs' and 'aaahs' and 'la-la-lahs,' ". then says, "As if on cue, the hoppers and twisters drop to their knees. A man from France curls up in a fetal position, burying his face in the carpet. . . . Here and there someone starts speaking in tongues" (pages 55, 56).

The article reported that Pentecostalism claims 20 million members in the United States and 225 million worldwide (page 56). The Bible gives a totally different picture of what it is like to be Spirit-filled. Galatians 5:22, 23 mention nine fruits of the Spirit—love, joy, peace, patience, kindness, goodness, faithfulness, gentleness, and self control. This suggests that being filled with the Spirit is the same as possessing the fruits of the Spirit. *To be Spirit-filled is to be filled with love. And joy. And peace. And self-control. And with the other qualities listed.*

Being Spirit-filled doesn't make a fool out of you. Rather, the Holy Spirit helps you act with compassion, in love, and with dignity.

MORE ABOUT THE FRUITS

In his book *Mighty Prevailing Prayer*, Wesley L. Duewel, describes the Spirit-filled person like this:

> In all other respects, theirs is a normal life—Spirit-filled, sanctified to God's will, and radiant with His presence and joy. They are not unbalanced, abnormal, or fanatical. They are not boasting of a superior spirituality. They are wholesomely normal in their home life, work life, and church life. But in the hidden place of prayer they have power with God and exercise the prayer authority of Christ's throne (page 51).

Pastor Duewel adds that the Spirit-filled person has a deep concern for the needs of the church and of all who hurt. He says this about them:

> Rivers of love, joy, peace, patience, and goodness flow out from their innermost being (John 7:38; Galatians 5:22, 23). They carry with them a special portion of God's presence, In them reside quiet power, intensity of commitment, active faith, and a disciplined and devoted life of prayer (Ibid.).

That's what I want! Do you also long for a full measure of these influences in your life?

LIKE A MOUNTAIN STREAM

Shortly before Jesus was crucified, He attended the Feast of Tabernacles—a yearly week-long festival at which there was much ceremony. By the last day of festivities the huge crowds had become weary. The celebrations did not satisfy the real heart-longings. Something was missing. Jesus entered the temple, and as He sensed the thirst in the hearts of the people, He said: "If anyone thirsts, let him come to Me and drink. He who believes in Me, as the Scripture has said, out of his heart will flow rivers of living water" (John 7:37, 38).

John explained what Jesus meant: "But this He spoke concerning the Spirit whom those believing in Him would receive" (John 7:39). In the Bible the Holy Spirit is also compared to dew (Hosea 14:5) and to rain (Zechariah 10:1). The Spirit refreshes, satisfies, and imparts life.

The heart that receives the Word of God and is filled with the Spirit becomes a channel for rivers of life. He or she becomes like a mountain stream that is "fed by unfailing springs, whose cool, sparkling waters leap from rock to rock, refreshing the weary, the thirsty, the heavy laden" (*Christ's Object Lessons,* page 130).

WELCOMING THE HOLY SPIRIT

The Holy Spirit is a person. In his book *The Spirit and His Church* Raymond Woolsey points out that in the New Testament the Holy Spirit has twenty-five different titles that indicate personality. He performs twenty different actions that only a personal being could carry out (page 12).

One time Ellen White told the students and faculty at Avondale College, "We need to realize that the Holy Spirit, who is as much a person as God is a person, is walking through these grounds" (*Evangelism,* page 616).

The Holy Spirit is as real and as loving as Christ Himself. If your eyes could be opened, you could see Him ready to walk through your front door to be with you in your home. If He is welcomed, the benefits are awesome. "The sweetest type of heaven is a home where the Spirit of the Lord presides" (*The Adventist Home,* page 15).

Are you comfortable with thinking of the Holy Spirit as a person? Are you welcoming Him into your heart and home? Here are three suggestions:

Think of the Holy Spirit both as a person and as a very special Friend

"I don't call you servants," Jesus said. "I call you friends" (see John 15:14, 15). The Holy Spirit likewise wants you for a very close friend.

Open your heart totally and completely to the Holy Spirit

Ask the Holy Spirit, as a precious Friend, to give you the mind of Christ (Philippians 2:5). Invite Him to help you love the things that Christ loves, and to hate the things that He hates. Invite Him to totally possess you—to guide your thoughts, your words, and your acts.

Spend much time with God's Word

Before opening God's Word, ask the Holy Spirit to enlighten your mind. Then as you read, remember that in every verse the Holy Spirit is speaking to you. His messages to you through the Word are as personal as if you heard an audible voice.

A SUGGESTED PRAYER

Wesley Duewel closes his book *Mighty Prevailing Prayer* with a suggested prayer. The following is a paragraph, slightly adapted, that I like to pray in moments of temptation, or when there is opportunity to renew my commitment to God.

> I give myself to You anew. Take me! Take all of me! Take me and fill me with Your Spirit so that it may not be I but You living in me, not my love but Your love pouring through me, not my power but Your mighty power working in and through me. Fill me so that it may not be I praying but your Spirit interceding through me (page 316).

I first wrote the preceding prayer on a 3-by-5 card, then kept the card with me until I had it over-learned. Now I can pray it when walking, driving, waiting in line, or whenever. It has done much to help me pray petitions that are more life-changing.

Why not give it a try?

TESTING IDEAS

Consider these ways to test one or more of the ideas in this chapter:

- *Could the rapid spread of Pentecostalism be the start of the false revival that takes place just before the return of Jesus? You might want to read the chapter in* The Great Controversy *titled "Modern Revivals."*
- *Analyze the preceding prayer from* Mighty Prevailing Prayer, *and if it appeals to you, write it on a 3-by-5 card to keep with you until you have it memorized. Try using it freely even as you memorize it.*

Chapter 8

A Passion to Fully Trust Him

"Trust God from the bottom of your heart;
don't try to figure everything out on your own.
Listen for God's voice in everything you do;
he's the one who will keep you on track."
(Proverbs 3:5, 6, The Message)

"I have trouble trusting God," said 22-year-old Deanna, who would be graduating from Andrews University with a degree in audiology in a few days. "I keep thinking, What now? I'm afraid to trust."

As we closed the 1997–98 school year, a prayer group that consisted mostly of seniors met for their last time. They had studied and prayed together almost every Thursday night at 8:30 p.m. since the start of their freshman year. Partway through their senior year Deanna Inman and Jonathan Brauer, two of the leaders, had asked me to become part of their group.

Jonathan led the final study. He had chosen a few paragraphs from *The*

Ministry of Healing chapter titled "Helps in Daily Living." He read about plans for the future, about wages, and about God's ability to provide.

Though soon to graduate, no one in the group had a promise of a job. After finishing the reading, Jonathan asked for comments. Carrie, the first to respond, said, "The whole chapter is awesome, especially for seniors."

Deanna spoke up, "I liked the part about letting God plan for you. I tend to worry, but if I would just trust God, life would become so simple."

Matt, another senior, asked Jonathan to reread this statement: "Many . . . have an anxious, troubled heart because they are afraid to trust themselves with God. They do not make a complete surrender to Him, for they shrink from the consequences that such a surrender may involve" (pages 480, 481).

Carrie, with uplifted hand, exclaimed, "That's me! I keep thinking, If I surrender, what's God going to make me do? I'm afraid it will be something I don't want to do. What also caught my attention was the comment about trying to reach the world's standard and with it adopting the world's customs."

THE CHALLENGE OF SURRENDER

Larra, a theology senior, said, "One thing that keeps me from total surrender to God is the way He sometimes answers my prayers. If I pray for patience, He gives me more trials. I wish He would give me a list of what He expects."

Then she continued thoughtfully, "Maybe what I most need is to pray for understanding."

"With final exams about to start," Carrie interjected, "I also worry about my grades and that keeps my eyes off Christ."

Matt suggested, "Ten thousand years from now not getting an "A" in everything won't matter a particle."

To that Deanna said, "It won't matter a year from now."

Deanna, for whom the quarter has been the hardest of her four years at Andrews, shared this: "Three weeks ago I quit setting my alarm. I let God wake me up. He usually does about 4:00 a.m."

She spoke, also, of attempting to get to bed earlier. On that I remembered an Ellen White statement my daughter had found when doing a research paper. It was this: "I know from the testimonies given me from time to time for brain workers, that sleep is worth far more before than after midnight. Two hours good sleep before twelve o'clock is worth more than four hours after twelve o'clock" (see *7 Manuscript Releases,* page *224*).

I mentioned this, and the scientific evidence that is starting to back it up.

Then Keri said, "I need to remember that God has a thousand ways to provide for us of which we know nothing. But when it comes to grades we need balance. We've got to do our part and not fool around when we should be studying."

Matt quoted Paul about the fact that it is in weakness we must trust God. "We don't learn until we fail," he said.

Carrie then added, "When it comes to failure, I need to keep asking, 'Where is it that I am not fully submitting to God?' "

SURRENDER AND TRUST

As these young adults made comments and shared personal experiences, this assurance from *Messages to Young People* came to mind: "The surrender of all our powers to God greatly simplifies the problems of life. It weakens and cuts short a thousand struggles with the passions of the natural heart" (page 30).

There are other benefits. Along with fewer struggles, these include:

- Peace that includes a perfect rest in God's love (Isaiah 26:3, 4; John 14:27).
- A sense of the Holy Spirit's presence (John 3:34; 14:16-18).
- The joys that come from being a "laborer together with God" (1 Corinthians 3:9).
- Completeness in Christ (Colossians 2:10).

You might want to underline these five words from Colossians 2:10, "You are complete in Him." The book *Education*, in the chapter titled "Faith and Prayer," has this comment, "Through faith in Christ, every deficiency of character may be supplied, every defilement cleansed, every fault corrected, and every excellence developed" (page 257).

CHRIST'S BLOOD AND FAITH

In chapter 5, "Brokenness at the Cross," I told of changed lives we saw at a prayer conference at Miracle Meadows, near Kalamazoo, Michigan. On that Sabbath afternoon more than an hour had been scheduled as free time. I took *30 Days to a More Powerful Prayer Life*, found a secluded place under a large tree, and reviewed all eight times in the book where I had directed attention to the blood of Christ.

In chapter 12 of *30 Days* I had included this assurance: "Every sincere prayer that is offered is mingled with the efficacy of Christ's blood. If the answer is deferred, it is because God desires us to show a holy boldness in claiming the pledged word of God" (*In Heavenly Places,* page 74).

In chapter 18 I noted that in *Incredible Answers to Prayer* Roger Morneau wrote that before bringing his prayer requests to the Lord he turns to the crucifixion scenes of Matthew 27. I then related that late in the summer of 1997 I went through that chapter looking for the word *blood,* and found blood mentioned five times (verses 4, 6, 8, 24, 25). Three more events brought blood, namely, the scourging, the crown of thorns pressed into Christ's scalp, and the crucifixion (verses 26, 30, 35).

Almost every day, I wrote, I either open my Bible to Matthew 27, or recall the eight times the word *blood* is in that chapter, and claim that blood in behalf of several groups: the children and youth of the church, denominational leaders, and all those open to becoming Spirit filled.

I then noted, in chapter 18, that mention of Christ's blood has a devastating effect on Satan. Volume 5 of the *Testimonies* contains a letter, "Praise Ye the Lord," written to a discouraged couple of the 1880s. In it Ellen White suggested, "When Satan would fill your mind with despondency, gloom, and doubt, resist his suggestions. Tell him of the blood of Jesus, that cleanses from all sin. You cannot save yourself from the tempter's power, but he trembles and flees when the merits of that precious blood are urged" (page 317).

I will never forget the blessings from spending an hour under that tree in prayer and in a focus on the blood of Christ. (If you have *30 Days,* and want to do something similar, the pages that mention Christ's blood are 25, 47, 60, 73, 76, 83, 88, and 105.)

In preparing this chapter, I noted that the context for the above statement about prayers being mingled with the efficacy of Christ's blood says this: "He is faithful who has promised. He will never forsake the soul who is wholly surrendered to Him" (Ibid.).

Total surrender blended with confidence in the blood of Christ! I want more and more and still more.

IDEAS TO TEST

As you think about the truths in this chapter, you might want to do one or more of the following:

- *Read Matthew 27, and write "blood" in the margin by each verse where the word is mentioned or implied. Then begin the habit of praying with your Bible open to that chapter.*

- The Living Bible paraphrases Colossians 2:10 like this: "You have everything when you have Christ." Have you found that to be true? Does faith in Christ provide for just about every spiritual need any person could have?
- In the statement about Satan fleeing when the merits of Christ's blood are urged, what significance do you see in the word urged?
- The book Education helped Seventh-day Adventists apply many of the Bible principles that governed the schools of the prophets to their school system. It contains a chapter entitled "Faith and Prayer." If you have access to it, or would want to purchase it from an Adventist Book Center, you'll find that chapter a real faith-builder.

Chapter 9

A Passion to Be Totally His

*"She will bring forth a Son, and you shall call His name Jesus,
for He shall save His people from their sins."*
(Matthew 1:21)

Call His name Jesus. On this mid-July 1998 Sunday afternoon I just finished interviewing a twenty-two-year-old woman who, until her baptism eight
months ago, faithfully practiced the Jewish faith. She is now enrolled at the
seminary at Andrews University. Her name is Michelle Zirkle, and she is here to
train to become a hospital chaplain.

I met her yesterday at the Seeds Conference, an annual church planting
seminar at Andrews. Sabbath morning Ruthie Jacobsen, the NAD Prayer and
Ministry Conference director, had a seminar about the method of Bible study
generally used at prayer conferences. After explaining the method, she divided

the sixty attendees into groups of eight, so each could experience that kind of Bible study. I ended up in the same group as Michelle.

Here's her story about her transition from being a devout Jew to an Adventist seminarian:

Pastor Joe: Michelle, how much did you know about Jesus when you were still Jewish in your faith?

Michelle: Almost nothing. I don't recall ever hearing His name at the synagogue. We were taught, if asked about Jesus, to say, "He was a great teacher, but not the Son of God." I knew so little about Jesus that when I heard the word Calvary, I had no idea what it was.

Pastor Joe: Are your parents both Jewish?

Michelle: No, Dad grew up Lutheran, and my mom Jewish. Her parents are Orthodox Jews, and Dad converted to the Jewish faith when he married Mom. In Hebrew homes we use the matriarchal system; all children born to a Jewish mother are Jews.

Pastor Joe: What led you to check out Christianity and Adventism?

Michelle: I was a senior at Indiana University, at Bloomington, majoring in human development and family studies. One day in April of 1997, I prayed, "God, would you cause something exciting to happen in my life today?"

Pastor Joe: What happened?

Michelle: I went to a shop to photocopy a class report. I met a law student named Tony who had been in the navy. We visited a bit, and the next day he called me and asked for a date.

During the date I found out he was a Christian, and I asked, "Why do you Christians teach that people go to heaven or hell at death? Scripture calls death a sleep. And as Jews we believe that no one is punished eternally."

"I believe that too," Tony said. "I'm a Seventh-day Adventist." He told me more about Seventh-day Adventist beliefs. I got real excited. The only Bible I had was the Pentateuch, so I asked Tony for a full Bible.

Pastor Joe: What happened next? When and how did you become a Seventh-day Adventist?

Michelle: Tony started taking me to the Wednesday night meetings at his church. I loved the people, and got acquainted with Pastor Donald Short. Tony had a lot of Doug Bachelor and Mark Finley videos, and we watched them.

When Mom saw I was getting interested, she insisted that I talk to our rabbi. I wrote out some questions, and Tony went with me. When I asked about the prophecies of Daniel, the rabbi quickly changed the subject. I left very dissatisfied.

Pastor Joe: Going back to your prayer in April of 1997, what would you say God gave you as something thrilling?

Michelle: Falling in love with Jesus. I would have never guessed, in a million years, that I would ever be in anything but Judaism. But now Jesus means everything to me. I was baptized on November 29, 1997. I love Him, I love Him.

Pastor Joe: Now you and Tony are married. Tell us about that.

Michelle: As Tony and I kept attending Bible studies, we became friends, then best friends. In October, he proposed to me. Pastor Short married us on April 11, one year and four days after we first met in the copy shop.

Pastor Joe: Why the Seminary?

Michelle: I had been feeling convicted that I should become a hospital chaplain, but I kept fighting it. Finally Tony said, Why not at least apply? Even though it was late to get here for this 1998 summer school, by a whole series of miracles we are here. Tony found a job over the state line into Indiana, and is able to take one class in the seminary.

Pastor Joe: What classes have you taken so far?

Michelle: For the first summer session, I took Christian History and Introduction to the Old Testament. This half I'm taking Introduction to Theology and Life and Ministry of Ellen G. White.

Pastor Joe: What's your reaction to the idea of a messenger such as Ellen White?

Michelle: Tony gave me *The Great Controversy.* I read the first two chapters, but was not familiar yet with Christian terms. Then he gave me *The Desire of Ages.* I read it, and loved it. I don't have the slightest doubt about God using her as a messenger.

WHY I LOVE JESUS

Let me shift from Michelle's testimony about her love for Jesus to my own. I became a Seventh-day Adventist as a teenager after taking the Voice of Prophecy Bible lessons. Back when I first taught my Workshop in Prayer class, I compiled a *Faith and Prayer Syllabus* that consisted of about one hundred one-page outlines. In the thirteen-page section "Getting Acquainted," I titled one of the outlines "Why I Love Him." Here's an abbreviated summary of the reasons I included:

He would have died for me alone (John 3:16; Luke 15:2-7)

If I were drowning, and someone saved me, I would be forever grateful. My Savior rules a vast universe of galaxies and supergalaxies and super-

supergalaxies. Yet He willingly, even eagerly, went to a horrible cross to save me.

He banishes darkness with light and hope (John 8:12)

If Jesus had not come, we would have known nothing but the horrors of darkness and the miseries of despair.

He sees me, not as I am, but as I can become—a new creation in Him (2 Corinthians 5:17)

The author of *Education* puts it like this: "In every human being He discerned infinite possibilities. He saw men as they might be, transfigured by His grace—in 'the beauty of the Lord our God' " (page 80).

He inspires me to believe I can reach His ideal for me (Matthew 9:10-13)

Sinners knew Jesus cared. "Looking on them with hope, He inspired hope. Meeting them with confidence, He inspired trust. Revealing in Himself man's true ideal, He awakened, for its attainment, both desire and faith" (*Education*, page 80).

Jesus Christ is the embodiment of everything admirable

"His name will be called Wonderful, Counselor, Mighty God, Everlasting Father, Prince of Peace" (Isaiah 9:6).

TOTALLY HIS

Do you see why I want to belong totally to Jesus Christ? Can you understand why, as mentioned in chapter 2, I want to love and live by every word that proceeds out of the mouth of God? Let me sum up my desires by two expressions: totally His, and living by every word.

Totally His

"You will seek Me, and find Me, when you search for Me with all your heart" (Jeremiah 29:13). Even in human relationships, that is reasonable and expected. No young man proposes to the girl he wants to marry by saying, "I love you with almost all of my heart; I'm saving one percent for a girl I dated before I met you."

For all of us, shouldn't *totally His* be true of the commitment we make to the One called "Altogether Lovely"?

Living by every word

Does the phrase of Jesus "every word" sound restrictive?

I have not found it to be oppressive in the slightest. Take Philippians 4:8, for example: "Finally, brethren, whatever things are true, whatever things are noble, whatever things are just, whatever things are pure, whatever things are lovely, whatever things are of good report, if there is any virtue and if there is anything praiseworthy, meditate on these things."

At first glance that sounds *very* restrictive. It shuts out a lot of TV, along with things like dancing, theater attendance, gambling, rock music, etc. But for every restriction in Scripture, God provides what the book *Education* calls "something better" (page 296).

Jesus said, "I have come that they may have life, and that they may have it more abundantly" (John 10:10). I have found that to be true, a thousand times over.

I want to live the totally Spirit-filled life described in chapter 7. I come far short of maintaining a total surrender every moment, but God keeps working with me as I seek that surrender.

USABLE IDEAS

"But you, beloved," Jude writes, "building yourselves up on your most holy faith, praying in the Holy Spirit, keep yourselves in the love of God" (verses 20, 21).

Here again is the prayer I introduced in chapter 7. It is adapted from Wesley Duewel's *Mighty Prevailing Prayer*:

I give myself to You anew. Take me! Take all of me! Take me and fill me with Your Spirit so that it may not be I but You living in me, not my love but Your love pouring through me, not my power but Your mighty power working in and through me. Fill me so that it may not be I praying but your Spirit interceding through me (page 316).

I love that last sentence! Isn't it what Jude talked about in verses 20 and 21 of his book? More and more I want to experience what it means to "pray in the Holy Spirit."

Here are some options for using ideas in this chapter:

- *Write a short testimony in which you give three or four reasons why you love Jesus. Then share it with a friend, or in a study group.*
- *When tempted to turn stones to bread, Jesus resisted by saying, "Man shall not live by bread alone, but by every word that proceeds from the mouth of God" (Matthew 4:4). Use these words when tempted by appetite or some other evil.*

Chapter 10

A Passion to Reflect Him

"Let the beauty of the Lord our God be upon us,
and establish the work of our hands for us;
Yes, establish the work of our hands."
(Psalm 90:17)

The beauty of the Lord our God. Of what does it consist? And does fragrance accompany beauty?

The June 15, 1998 issue of *Time* magazine had an article about the $5 billion perfume industry. At an event in Manhattan's Lincoln Center, hundreds of well-dressed women had just paid $950 a ticket to attend a black-tie awards event sponsored by the Fragrance Foundation.

The attendees sat under a marquee spelling "THAT'S SCENTERTAINMENT." Those who attended went around asking one another, "Do you like my fragrance?"

Cruden's Complete Concordance begins with a page that lists references for some 140 names or titles for Christ. Each represents some aspect of His character. Two of those are "Rose of Sharon" and "Lily of the Valley," both of which imply fragrance.

Would you like for your family, friends, and neighbors to see "the beauty of the Lord our God" in your character and personality? And how about a reflection of Him in your face?

The dictionary defines character, when applied to people, as traits or qualities, such as compassion, self-discipline, fortitude, etc. Personality is broader and takes in not only qualities but also one's emotional makeup, feelings, and personal attractiveness.

It's as Christ becomes more and more a part of your character and personality that your face radiates Him.

INFLUENCE AS A PERFUME

In a statement about influence, Paul wrote, "None of us lives to himself" (Romans 14:7). And in 2 Corinthians he uses the word fragrance twice to describe Christian influence: "Now thanks be to God who always leads us in triumph in Christ, and through us diffuses the fragrance of His knowledge in every place, For we are to God the fragrance of Christ among those who are being saved and among those who are perishing" (2 Corinthians 2:14, 15).

The book *Christ's Object Lessons* has a chapter titled "Talents." It contains practical applications drawn from the parable of the talents in Matthew 25. Are you sometimes tempted to think you have no talents with which to share the gospel? Here are eight specific talents discussed one at a time: mental faculties, speech, influence, time, health, strength, money, and kindly impulses and affections.

The author has interesting things to say about all eight, but space limits us to a discussion of only one: influence. This paragraph talks about something some don't realize they have: an "atmosphere" that surrounds them: "Every soul is surrounded by an atmosphere of its own—an atmosphere, it may be, charged with the life-giving power of faith, courage, and hope, and sweet with the fragrance of love" (page 339).

Haven't you known people like that? When you are with them, their faith and courage and hope and love infect you. They are examples of the fragrance Paul wrote about.

The same paragraph mentions another kind of influence: "Or it may be heavy and chill with the gloom of discontent and selfishness or poisonous with the deadly taint of cherished sin" (Ibid.).

That's another kind of odor! Have you ever had a sack of potatoes that has been around so long a few have rotted? Isn't the smell awful?

Here's the punch line in the influence paragraph: "By the atmosphere surrounding us, every person with whom we come in contact is consciously or unconsciously affected" (Ibid.).

The next paragraph makes an application:

"This is a responsibility from which we cannot free ourselves. Our words, our acts, our dress, our deportment, even the expression of the countenance, has an influence. Upon the impression thus made there hang results for good or evil which no man can measure" (Ibid., pages 339, 340).

Then come two sentences about character: "Character is power. The silent witness of a true, unselfish, godly life carries an almost irresistible influence" (page 340).

An almost irresistible influence! That's one of the benefits from seeking to become a Spirit-filled godly young person, or old person, or anyone in between.

A POWERFUL BEHAVIORAL LAW

One of the most powerful spiritual laws in human experience can be stated in this five-word summary of what Paul writes in 2 Corinthians 3:18—"By beholding we become changed." And that is true not only in character. It can also work with people who need to be more neat in dress, or more attentive in their work, or more diligent in the classroom.

In the book Morning Riser Walter R. L. Scragg tells this story: An unkempt little girl wandered into an art gallery where beautiful landscapes and portraits were displayed. Entranced, she went from one to another. Suddenly, she stopped before a picture of a lovely young woman. She feasted her eyes on the clothes and on the sweet, beautiful face of the person in the picture.

The girl glanced at her own ragged dress and dirty feet and hands. As she looked back at the portrait, her hand strayed to her own untidy hair. Finally she turned and went out to the street.

The next day she was back. An attendant, noticing her intense interest in the painting, said to her, "She's lovely, isn't she?"

"Sir," the girl replied, "she's not just lovely, she's the most beautiful person I have ever seen. Who is she?"

"She's a princess," the attendant replied. "A great artist painted her for the king."

The following day she was there again. The attendant noticed that her dress had been mended; her hair shone from vigorous brushing; her feet were clean. Again she stared wistfully into the face of the young woman in the picture.

As the days went by, the attendant saw changes in the girl's face. The influence of beauty had transformed her. She was no longer a street urchin, but a sweet young lady, tidy and clean.

HIS MATCHLESS ATTRACTIONS

In my Workshop in Prayer class at Andrews University, near the start of a new quarter I sometimes ask each student in the class to mention the one quality in Jesus that he or she most admires. I invite someone to put each name on a chalkboard, and at times the class has come up with enough qualities to fill the board.

One quality that generally gets included is approachability—a quality not often seen in human leaders. Abraham Lincoln had it, though. F. B. Carpenter, in his 1887 book The Inner Life of Abraham Lincoln: Six Months at the White House, wrote this about Abraham Lincoln: "Nothing was more marked in Mr. Lincoln's personal demeanor than his unconsciousness of his position" (page 95).

Lincoln had been elevated from an unknown in a country town to the dignities and duties of the Presidency. Carpenter wrote it would be difficult, if not impossible, to find another man who wouldn't feel it necessary "to assume something of the manner and tone befitting that position" (Ibid.).

Lincoln didn't. Neither did Jesus. He carried with Him no aura of importance. He had no desire to make a name for Himself. When He said, "I do not seek my own glory" (John 8:50), none of His critics could contradict that statement.

He's still the same. Jesus has kept His human body, scars and all. Throughout the eternity of the past—as He "hung the worlds in space"—He needed only speak "and it was done" (Psalm 33:9) Yet as you visit with Him by the river of life, He will seem more like a much-loved older brother than an Intergalactic Executive and Co-Creator who runs this universe of billions of clusters of galaxies and supergalaxies.

USABLE IDEAS

Here are a few options to consider as you think about what this chapter might offer for becoming more Spirit-filled:

- *When it comes to praying for someone—a child, friend (or enemy if any)— to develop a good character, there probably is no better prayer than the one in bold print at the start of this chapter. If you are ready to start memorizing another prayer, write Psalm 90:16 on a 3-by-5 card, and begin including it in our prayers.*
- *Had you realized that an invisible "atmosphere" surrounds you and affects every person you spend time with?*
- *"By beholding we become changed." How can a parent take advantage of this behavioral law?*

Chapter 11

A Passion for Oneness With Our Father

*"To you who believe,
He is precious."*
(1 Peter 2:7)

The preceding words were penned by Peter about our Savior. In this chapter I want to tell why for me *precious* also applies to our heavenly Father, and why I adore Him.

As a child, did you feel close to your dad? I didn't. He had come from a hard-working German ancestry where children were helpers for getting the farm work done, and he seldom expressed any kind of affection. He had also waited until almost forty to marry, which added an age barrier.

In similar fashion, the fathers in millions of homes today spend so much time with career responsibilities that they are seldom able to build good bonds with their children. In other homes single moms are trying to be both Mom and Dad. To say God is like a father doesn't always attract people to Him.

Where, then, do children get good feelings about God as a father? Consider these two Bible truths:

- Along with "Wonderful" and "Counselor" a Messianic prophecy calls Jesus "Everlasting Father" (Isaiah 9:6)
- Jesus said, "He who has seen Me has seen the Father" (John 14:9). He came to this planet as "the Son of man," with a heart that loved children and all who have been neglected or exploited.

For an example, watch as He cleanses the temple on the Sunday afternoon before His crucifixion. Terrified, money-changers and Pharisees flee, but as you stand watching, you notice the people who didn't—the blind, the deaf, the lame, and lots of children. They crowd about Jesus, and He heals every cripple, every ill child.

He then seats Himself, and begins to teach. After a time, He picks up a little one that has timidly come up to Him. She leans against the breast of Christ, and goes to sleep. Jesus makes room on His lap for a second little one, perhaps a blind boy that He has just healed. The child, filled with wonder, looks intently at the kindly face of Jesus.

Jesus pauses, and several delighted children begin to sing. Others join them. Soon "Hosanna to the Son of David" fills the temple court (Matthew 21:14-16). You watch as an Intergalactic Executive tenderly holds two children on His lap.

Our Father is like that too!

A THIRTEEN-YEAR-OLD'S FATHER

Consider a pen picture, as told by Sharon Cress in the June 1996 issue of *Ministry* magazine. Sharon grew up in a small Florida community where the town celebrated Founders Day every February. The year she turned thirteen the parade committee invited her and others to ride their horses in the procession.

"Although flattered," she said, "I was also scared. My new horse, a jet-black Tennessee walking mare named Midnight, was spirited and magnificent, and a little too much horse for a ninety-pound adolescent."

Sharon's father told her that with his guidance, she could handle the challenge. "It wouldn't be easy," she thought. "Midnight sensed that she had intimidated me, and the couple of times that she had run away with me bruised both ego and body. Riding her around the lane at our farm was one thing. Controlling her along a noisy parade route was quite another. Yet this was an opportunity I didn't want to miss."

The crisp morning air on the day of the parade made Midnight more frisky. As Sharon waited in the lineup, her father sensed her apprehension and told her, "You'll do fine. I will see you at the end of the parade." As the parade started, Sharon said, the four-mile route seemed like forty.

"I was afraid to take my eyes, even for a few seconds, away from the mare's ears and head. I needed to know every second how she was coping with the pandemonium around us. Horns honked. People shouted. Children ran into the street. I needed to keep close control of the situation. Step by high step, Midnight finally seemed to settle down a bit and enjoy the attention and admiration of the downtown crowd."

WAS THAT DAD?

To Sharon the mass of people on both sides seemed like a blur. But then she thought she saw her father behind the crowd. "Several minutes later," she said, "I dared to look up at the people again. It seemed as if I were hallucinating, because there he was again—showing up everywhere.

"A few minutes later it looked like him again behind another cluster of people. Again and again, as I maneuvered down the street, I caught glimpses of him in the sunlight and in the shadows of the downtown buildings.

"When we finally reached our own crowded yard near the end of the parade route, Daddy stood in the front yard. There he was to meet us as he had promised."

In her surprise, Sharon told him, "I thought I saw you about twenty times along the parade route. Were you there?"

"Yes," he smiled. "I ran the whole parade route behind the crowds just to make sure you were OK. I never let you out of my sight for a second." Then he joked, "It was the only way your mother would give permission for you to ride today."

Sharon drew this parallel: "Sometimes it seems we are out there alone in the crowd. But then, in a still moment, when we dare look away from trying to control the situations ourselves, when we tune out the distractions, we get a glimpse of Him. He is actually right there, perhaps in the background, running along beside us, feeling every insecurity, ensuring our safety, watching over us every moment."

Amen and Amen!

APPROACHING OUR FATHER IN PRAYER

In *Mighty Prevailing Prayer* Wesley Duewel attempts to picture the delight God takes in us when we come to Him in prayer. "Your prayer time," he suggests, "is always a joy time to the Lord" (page 46). He's especially delighted when we come with a burden to pray for His other children.

"The eyes of the Lord," I pointed out in chapter 2, "run to and fro throughout the whole earth, to show Himself strong on behalf of those whose heart is loyal to Him" (2 Chronicles 16:9). He is especially looking for youth and others whom He can fill with His Spirit, and with a passion to bring lost people to Jesus.

In that same chapter I told of my dream that by the year 2001 God will have raised up at least 100,000 youth—and that many leaders and laymen—who are totally surrendered to Him. In praying for youth I know—the Larras, the Williams, the Ricks, the Jonathans, the Philips, the Delindas, the Rochelles, the Yvonnes, the Jennifers, the Arts—I sense that my heart throbs in unison with the heart of my heavenly Father.

I love the few I know of the youth God is raising up, and I see them as a symbol of the tens of thousands I don't know. I know my heavenly Father loves them a thousand times more fervently than I or their parents or anyone else can. That very fact gives me very tender feelings about my Father.

Paul speaks of our being laborers together with God (1 Corinthians 3:9). It's a partnership, as if God is saying to me and to each reader of this book, "I'll do the searching; you do the praying. Your prayers give Me the right to do more than I could do without your fervent intercessions."

Will you join me? Your sense of partnership with our Father will make Him very precious to you.

THE MIGHTY PLEA OF CHRIST'S BLOOD

I almost never pray without mentioning the blood of Christ. Over recent months my favorite intercessory prayer has become the one that begins, "Our Father in heaven."

The Lord's Prayer has three kingdom requests, and three requests for personal needs. I see it as an outline to which we can add other Bible statements, or words of our own. In my classes, and in private intercession, I urge adding this phrase, "Because of the blood of Jesus."

Here's how I love to pray it in behalf of youth and others I long to see become Spirit-filled.

- *That God's name be hallowed and respected.* On this request I begin, "Because of the blood of Christ, please hallow Your name in the lives of those You are raising up. Fill them with Your Spirit *today* so that it is You living in them."
- *That God's kingdom come.* I ask, "Because of the blood of Jesus may Your kingdom of grace work powerfully in their lives *today*. Bless them and make them a blessing."
- *That God's will be done.* I plead, "Father, because of the blood Jesus shed on Calvary, may *Your* will become their great passion. Fulfill your will in their lives *today*. Help them put self aside and live a life wholly consecrated to You."

On these kingdom requests, I emphasize *today*. I draw this from Paul's use of *now* (2 Corinthians 6:2). I think God is pleased, when we ask that His name be hallowed, that we urge Him to act, not a year from now, but *now*. We may not see what He did until eternity, but when we get urgent, I believe it gives Him the right to do more and still more *now*.

I then go to the three personal needs in the Lord's Prayer. These I generally put in the context of gratitude, like this:

- *Give us this day our daily bread.* For this I say, "Thank you that because of Your blood we have daily bread, shelter, clothes, and other needs. Help us—and all youth—to realize that every loaf of bread comes stamped with the cross of Calvary."
- *Forgive our debts as we forgive others.* "Precious Father, there on the cross, as Christ's blood fell to the rocks below, He asked forgiveness for His murderers. Please bless us with that same spirit. Make us willing, eager, to forgive others seven times seventy if need be. Give us a determination to watch and pray, lest we fall into more sin."
- *Lead us not into temptation, but deliver from the evil within and from the Evil One without.* I add, "Please, Father, Christ's blood gives you the right to do this. Thank You, thank You!"

A FINAL BLOW TO SATAN

In doing this I often rely on a Bible statement that mentions the blood of Christ. One I just started using is 1 Peter 1:2, which reads: "Elect according to the foreknowledge of God the Father, in sanctification of the Spirit for obedience and sprinkling of the blood of Jesus Christ."

I then end the Lord's Prayer like this: "Because of the blood of Jesus, Yours is the kingdom, and the power, and the glory forever. Thank You, Father, that the blood of Christ gives You the right to claim the youth of the church as part of Your kingdom. That blood gives you the power to transform each one, and that blood brings glory to Your name through transformed lives. Amen and Amen!"

As a final blow to Satan, I often cite the sentence from volume 5 of the *Testimonies for the Church,* that Satan "trembles and flees when the merits of that precious blood are urged" (page 317). I take the word *urged* and really press it home to our precious heavenly Father. I can spend several minutes just on that fact: *Satan trembles and flees when we urge the blood of Christ in behalf of the children, youth, or whoever we want under the cover of His blood.* I believe God is pleased, delighted, when we do this, for it gives Him the right to work with a power Satan can't resist.

THINGS TO TRY

Here are some suggestions which may help you to test ideas presented in this chapter:

- *In the story of thirteen-year-old Sharon, imagine yourself as her. What would have been your feelings about your father at the end of the parade?*
- *For the next few days try praying the Lord's Prayer as described in this chapter. Then, if you have opportunity, teach another person to pray it with you in that manner.*

Chapter 12

A Passion for God's Word

"Therefore every teacher . . . who has been instructed
about the kingdom of heaven is like
the owner of a house who brings out of his storeroom
new treasures as well as old."
(Matthew 13:52, NIV)

When Jesus gave His Sermon by the Sea, recorded in Matthew 13, He told eight stories—parables—and closed with the above as His final one. See if you agree with this interpretation:

Owner of the house: one of us
Storeroom: the Scriptures
New treasures: new facts, ideas, and insights derived from a study of God's Word
Old treasures: Bible facts and ideas already known and from which new applications of truth can be gained

House with a treasure storeroom suggests a place where things of great value are kept. My dictionary defines *treasure* as (1) accumulated or stored wealth, especially in the form of money, precious metals, jewels, etc., (2) any person or thing considered very valuable.

Gold is one of the most sought-after of non-people treasures. Here's a story I often share with students:

During gold rush days, Sonora, California, was a region where miners sometimes struck it rich. Every day treasure seekers headed into the surrounding hills to look for gold, using a road constructed of rocks and gravel. One day after a heavy rain a man led his mule, pulling a cart, up the steep road. "Whoa!" he cried, reining his mule to a halt. Grimacing with pain, he looked with disgust at the rock over which he had stumbled.

"Wish they wouldn't use such big rocks in the roads," he muttered. "With rains like the one last night they get washed loose and can be dangerous." With that he bent down to hoist it to the side.

"Just a minute!" he whistled to himself as he took a second look. "This is no ordinary rock." He lifted it into the cart to examine more carefully. "Gold if I ever saw it!" he exclaimed, staring in awe at the rock he had just found. It was. Solid gold. Twenty-five pounds of it.

PEOPLE TREASURES

The second kind of treasure is a person or object considered to be valuable. As an illustration of that kind of treasure, I want to introduce you to Yvonne, a college sophomore. She has become a precious treasure through the life-changing power of the Word of God.

I met Yvonne at a Prayer Conference held at Andrews University the first weekend of April 1988. People were assigned to small group Bible study by numbering off, and I along with eight students ended up in the group led by her. The study topic was the prodigal son.

I was called out shortly after the study started. When I returned an hour later, the group had just finished. The AAA method of Bible study generally used (described in chapter 5) focuses on a passage with which you do three things—ask, answer, apply. "Yvonne," I said, "could you give me a two-minute summary of the things your group came up with under apply?"

To which she replied, "Do have two hours?" As often happens at a prayer conference, even familiar stories become rich with practical new insights.

Yvonne had attended the Berrien Springs High School. Since becoming a Christian a year ago, she has had a burden to reach her high school friends with the gospel, and each week she and her friend Tahani conduct Bible studies at the school. In contrast to what she used to be, she's totally into God's Word and into sharing it. Here's her testimony:

I was dedicated to the church as a baby and raised an Adventist. But as I reached high school, Satan drew me away from the Lord step by step. I tried to read the Bible but never got past the begats. I also wanted to have a relationship with Christ and be baptized, but I was a public school kid and didn't know who to ask.

Most of my friends were not Adventists, and I felt safe with them because they had Christian backgrounds. But eventually we began to experiment with drugs—tabacco, alcohol, marijuana, and LSD. During an LSD trip I became afraid I would lose my sanity and promised God that if He kept me sane I wouldn't do it again. But I did and bought one of the devil's lies, that I was unworthy of God's help. I didn't understand that the precious blood of Christ has paid our debt and that His Spirit can help us overcome sin.

I started taking massage classes in Kalamazoo, but I learned more than massage. I was introduced to the New Age, subtly, slowly, so that I didn't recognize it for what it was. When I finally did recognize it, I thought it would lead me to a better understanding of God.

As a child I feared the devil more than anything. I was afraid he would "get me." In my fear I doubted that God would do anything to help. I didn't realize that when we feel most alone, God's watch-care continues full-on!

As I began to study more of the philosophy at the massage school, I became comfortable thinking there was no devil. Eventually I had no clear idea what God was like either. In the books I read, God became a collection of souls spinning out in the universe waiting to be reincarnated. God was no longer the personal being I had known as a girl.

I attended some Insight Seminars put on by a New Age group in a rented church. They were advertised as a way to increase self-esteem and get more of what you want in life and less of what you don't want. I felt my fear of evil vanish, along with my sense of guilt.

My whole life focused on what I was learning. I memorized information from astrology books and numerology books I found at the library. I began preparing readings for people whose lives I was going to change by sharing these new truths with them.

I began a routine of daily affirmations which I thought would bring wealth and other things I wanted. I journaled about my dreams and searched them for the messages from what I thought was my higher self. I also became eager to interpret other people's dreams. Life started to seem like it had great purpose and meaning.

I was told that we choose our parents, and are here to teach them.

My two best friends, Amy and Heather, became equally involved, and supported my new belief system. My family, especially my dad and cousin Marcy, didn't. They confronted me with biblical truths. Forgetting what I had learned about the Bible as a child, I told them, "That's your truth, not mine." I continued to read many New Ages books instead of searching the Bible. But just as my friends and I were about to dive deeper into the dreadful sea of sin, the Lord started opening our eyes.

DELIVERANCE!

One day an instructor, who supposedly could "see auras" (hidden things) about me, told me that something awful was going to happen to me. She gave me no hope of redemption or of protection from this thing she foretold. I was scared and confused and went to talk to my friend Amy.

After a long talk about our New Age beliefs and teachers, we decided to seek out books that would tell us if we were in a cult. One book we found, by Will Barron, was called *Deceived by the New Age*. After reading and discussing it, we felt we needed to know Jesus. That led us to the Bible.

We then decided we wanted nothing more to do with the New Age. We gathered all our astrology and numerology books, our journals and notebooks, and drove to a field near Benton Harbor to burn them.

Our faces grew red from the flames as we threw book after book on the fire. We prodded the brilliant mass with broken branches, and exposed everything to the flames. It was as if we were burning the lies in our minds. All that we had based our lives upon became ashes. The smoke rose up as a symbol to Heaven, and we were grateful for a new beginning.

When the fire finally burned out, we got into the car. God spoke to us through a song on the radio, "Bridge Over Troubled Waters." As we listened, tears rolled down our cheeks. We had no idea what we would do next, but we had each other, and most important, we had God.

Since my conversion and baptism, God has given me many opportunities to share my testimony. I have new understandings of God's mercy. He wasn't angry with me for my weakness but longed for me to know His love.

I understand, also, the importance of Bible study and how easy it is for those who aren't grounded in the Word to be swept away by the intrigue of the New Age philosophy. If I had known how to study God's Word and how to develop a relationship with Him, I would have seen the lies in it.

I love this assurance from Hebrews: "Therefore do not cast away your confidence, which has great reward. For you have need of endurance, so that after you have done the will of God, you may receive the promise" (Hebrews 10:35, 36).

WONDERS OF THE BIBLE

Yvonne's experience illustrates these wonders found in the Bible:

- It reveals a God of love who keeps His eye of love on us even when we have been deceived, and by His providences He works continually to bring us back to Himself.
- As we study the Word of God we learn about the forgiveness that God freely offers when we come to the foot of the cross.
- Through Bible study God gives us a new heart, and helps us see tremendous meaning in life.
- The more we study the Bible, the more we want to share its wonderful truths with others.
- Even in the well-known stories, like the one of the prodigal son, we can never exhaust the truths they contain.

FOR DISCUSSION, OR FURTHER STUDY:

- *You might want to take another look at Matthew 13:52. Does the interpretation given at the start of this chapter make sense to you?*
- *What would it take, do you think, for you to find new insights almost every day as you study the Bible?*
- *Compare the bonfire story from this chapter with the Ephesus bonfire described in Acts 19:13-20, at which $10,000 worth (in today's measure) of magic and sorcery books went up in flames. If your family were to make a check of books, videos, and tapes for those that you could not ask God to bless, would a bonfire be in order? Before deciding, check Philippians 4:8.*
- *If the idea appeals to you, in your morning devotions keep a "something new" journal for a week. Or, if you can arrange for four or five others to join you for a small group study using the AAA method of Bible study, give it a try. For a description of the method, see chapter 5.*

Chapter 13

Blessings From Ellen White's Writings

*"And the dragon was enraged with the woman,
and he went to make war with the rest of her offspring,
who keep the commandments of God
and have the testimony of Jesus."*
(Revelation 12:17)

Have you been impacted by the twelfth chapter of Revelation? Could you interpret the above verse? Who is the dragon? Who is the woman that the dragon hates and would like to destroy? What's the war all about?

One Sunday afternoon an eleventh-grade boy took his Bible to the front porch and opened it to the book of Revelation. He had never heard of Seventh-day Adventists, and had known nothing of Bible prophecy, but now he had just finished the Voice of Prophecy Bible course.

That Sunday afternoon, as he tried to read the book of Revelation, he understood almost nothing. "Why not write the Voice of Prophecy and ask for help," he thought to himself.

Return mail brought a copy of Uriah Smith's *Daniel and the Revelation*. With growing fascination he read about the dragon, beasts, earthquakes, a bottomless pit, a city in the sky, a new earth. He learned that almost everything prophesied in both Daniel and Revelation has already happened, and that we now live in the last moments of the war between Christ and Satan that Revelation tells about.

Life would never be the same for that young man. New goals came into focus. There was a new road to travel. If he stayed on that road, it would take him all the way to the New Jerusalem of Revelation's last two chapters.

I was that farm boy. I learned that the dragon in the above verse is Satan, and that the woman represents the church from the time of Christ to the present time. The rest of her offspring, called the remnant in the King James Version, represents a called-out remnant that would take the messages of Revelation 14 to the entire globe just before Jesus returns.

This remnant has two identifying characteristics:

- It keeps the Ten Commandments
- It possesses a gift called the testimony of Jesus—something that Revelation 19 defines as "the spirit of prophecy" (Revelation 19:10).

A SAILBOAT RIDE

On a beautiful April day the captain of a large sailboat headed out through the Golden Gate onto the Pacific. The water was choppy, and several became seasick. One who didn't later wrote:

> Yesterday, Brother [Charles] Chittendon took out a number of us on the water in his boat. . . . We remained on the water and beach all day. Sailed out of the Golden Gate upon the ocean. . . . The waves ran high and we were tossed up and down so very grandly. . . . The spray dashing over us. The watchful captain giving his orders, the hands ready to obey. The wind was blowing strong and I never enjoyed anything as much in my life (*This Day With God*, page 110).

The woman? Someone who has written more books than any woman in history—counting the compilations, over one hundred titles now in print. She helped launch a health-care system that now numbers hundreds of clinics and hospitals. The educational system she helped begin now numbers 81 colleges and universities, 930 secondary schools, and some 4,500 elementary schools.

Some fifty printing presses help publish her materials. The church she helped start now numbers ten million, with members in almost all of earth's 236 countries.

The author, of course, was Ellen White. The secret of her life can be summed up in these words: "I want to know the will of God and do it. . . . I want all that I have and am to be used in the cause of God and to the glory of His name" (Letter 140, 1894).

One of her books, *Steps to Christ*, has been published in more than one hundred forty languages. The next two most widely read books are *The Great Controversy* and *The Desire of Ages*. During the time I studied their Bible lessons, the Voice of Prophecy sent a booklet every month—one such as Taylor Bunch's *Behold the Man*.

At the public high school that I attended in Newkirk, Oklahoma, the English teacher sought to instill in her students a love for good literature and had us memorize things like "Trees" and "To a Waterfowl." *Behold the Man* had numerous quotations from *The Desire of Ages*—quotes with a beauty like I had never read. I said to myself, "I need to get that book."

Another month the VOP sent the *Impending Conflict*—a booklet with the last ten chapters of *The Great Controversy*. I found it so fascinating I couldn't lay it down. It gripped me like no other book or booklet I have ever read.

THE WAR BEHIND WAR

At sixteen, I was baptized at the Oklahoma camp meeting. A favorite spot for me was the book tent. To my joy I found both *The Desire of Ages* and *The Great Controversy*, and bought both of them. I loved *The Desire of Ages*, and it and *The Great Controversy* helped hold me steady as I finished my senior year in public school.

A businessman in South America once said, "I wouldn't take a million dollars for *The Great Controversy* if I couldn't get another one." That's about how I feel too.

In an article titled "Caught in the Line of Fire" the July 13, 1998, issue of *Newsweek* featured the attention being given to books and movies about World War II. The article attempts to show the horrors of D-Day in Europe, when on June 6, 1944, allied forces hit Normandy Beach as the start of the invasion of Hitler's Fortress Europe. "The Allied victory was anything but certain," *Newsweek* said.

After General Dwight Eisenhower gave the go-ahead for the first of 10,000 planes and 5,000 ships to launch the attack, he sat down and drafted a statement to issue in case the invasion failed. He wrote: "Our landings . . . have failed to gain a satisfactory foothold and I have withdrawn the troops. If any blame or fault attaches to the attempt it is mine alone."

If the Normandy landings had failed, *Newsweek* said, the Allied attempt to rescue Western Europe could have been delayed indefinitely, and "the United States could have been forced to drop atomic bombs not on Hiroshima or Nagasaki but on Berlin and Frankfurt."

Hitler's scientists sought desperately to develop atomic bombs first. Had Germany succeeded, the first such bombs could have been dropped on London, Moscow, and maybe even smuggled into New York and exploded there.

I was in my middle teens during World War II, with no knowledge of Scripture until the Voice of Prophecy Bible lessons came to our home shortly after the end of the war. I still have most of the thirty-six senior Bible course lessons that changed my life forever. The first two lessons are missing, but lesson three, titled "Satan's Origin and Destiny," has the date Oct. 31, 1945, stamped on the answer sheet.

That lesson has four sections: "The Author of Sin," "Satan Originally in Heaven," "Satan Unmasked," and "The Controversy Ended." You cannot even begin to imagine the impact the content made on me, a religiously-ignorant Oklahoma farm lad, when I first read it just two months after the bombs were dropped on Hiroshima and Nagasaki!

UNPRECEDENTED EXCITEMENT

Not long after that I got the book *The Impending Conflict*, and then the full *Great Controversy*. Even in writing about it I have to fight to hold back tears of joy and excitement. And speaking of excitement, nothing in all literature equals the drama in the chapter in that book titled "God's People Delivered." Here's a description of the earthquake told about in Revelation 16:17-21:

There is a roar as of a coming tempest. The sea is lashed into fury. There is heard the shriek of a hurricane, like voices of demons on a mission of destruction. The whole earth heaves and swells like the waves of the sea. Its surface is breaking up Its very foundations seem to be giving way. Mountain chains are sinking. Inhabited islands disappear. The seaports that have become like Sodom for wickedness are swallowed by the angry waters (*The Great Controversy*, page 637).

The resurrection is described this way:

Amid the reeling of the earth, the flash of lightning, and the roar of thunder, the voice of the Son of God calls forth the sleeping saints. He looks upon the graves of the righteous, and then raising His hands to heaven, He cries, 'Awake, awake, awake, ye that sleep in the dust, and arise!' Throughout the length and breadth of the earth the dead shall hear that voice, and they that hear shall live (Ibid., page 644).

For understanding the issues about the warfare between Christ and Satan, as pictured in Revelation, nothing equals *The Great Controversy*. And for a biography of Christ that will help you love Him more and more, nothing ever penned equals *The Desire of Ages*. These two books are part of Ellen White's Conflict of the Ages series. This five-volume set of books covers all of earth's history, from Creation to the earth made new.

A TREASURE-FILLED SERIES

Altogether there are more than one hundred life-changing books written by Ellen White or compiled from her writings. These include books on just about any Bible, family, health, or devotional topic. Space permits mention of just one group: the morning devotional books.

In 1949 a book of devotional readings for each day of the year, taken from Ellen White's writings, with a Bible verse accompanied with comments, began to be published every third year. I just opened that first one, *With God at Dawn*, and found I had underlined this sentence: "Love is unsuspecting, ever placing the most favorable construction upon the motives and acts of others" (page 182). That one sentence could reduce a lot of heartache in families! And the book is filled with hundreds of such comments.

In my Workshop in Prayer class students purchase another such book called *In Heavenly Places*. To help them develop a habit of daily readings, each student is required to read a page each day; my hope is that they will continue to do so. Here's a brief sample of the hundreds of gems in that compilation:

Comment on "God is love" (1 John 4:8, 9)
"Christ's sacrifice for fallen man has no parallel. It is the most exalted, sacred theme on which we can meditate. Every heart that is enlightened by the grace of God is constrained to bow with inexpressible gratitude and adoration

before the Redeemer for His infinite sacrifice" (page 14).

Comment on "mighty to save" (Isaiah 63:1)
"Cast yourself wholly on His mercy. There is no difficulty within or without that cannot be surmounted in His strength. . . . Have faith in God. Trustful dependence on Jesus makes victory not only possible, but certain" (page 17).

Comment on "casting all your care upon Him" (1 Peter 5:7)
"No one who comes to Him goes away unhelped. Take your burdens to the divine Burden Bearer and leave them with Him, knowing that He will carry them for you. . . . There is no limit to the help that the Savior is willing to bestow on us" (page 275).

CHECKING THINGS OUT
With all God's gifts, the ultimate test is "Taste and see" (Psalm 34:8). For those new to the Adventist Church, here are three suggestions about where you might want to begin.

- *If you are new to the Adventist Church and haven't read* Steps to Christ, *by all means start with this little volume. The first six chapters are mostly about steps leading to a decision for Christ, and the last seven about how to grow in Christ. As you read, you may want to use a pencil and mark ideas you want to remember.*
- *A five-volume set by Ellen White, "The Conflict of the Ages," covers the Bible story from beginning to end. The books are* Patriarchs and Prophets, Prophets and Kings, The Desire of Ages, The Acts of the Apostles, *and* The Great Controversy. *You will enjoy each, but many start with* The Desire of Ages.
- *For more information about what the Bible teaches about the prophetic gift, see chapter 17, "The Gift of Prophecy," in the book* Seventh-day Adventists Believe . . . .

Chapter 14

A Passion for Prayer

"Here are my directions: Pray much for others;
plead for God's mercy upon them;
give thanks for all he is going to do for them."
(1 Timothy 2:1, The Living Bible)

Notice Paul's three imperatives: *Pray much* for others. *Plead for God's mercy* upon them. *Give thanks* for all God is going to do for them.

The preceding was written to a young man. Paul loved Timothy so much that he thought of him as his own son, and said this about praying for him:

Every time I say your name in prayer—which is practically all the time—I thank God for you . . . I miss you a lot, especially when I remember that last tearful goodbye, and I look forward to a joy-packed reunion (2 Timothy 1:3, 4, The Message).

That reunion never took place; Nero ordered Paul executed shortly after this. At the Second Coming, wouldn't you like to be where Paul will be as he and Timothy embrace?

Could I make a suggestion to pastors, teachers, and to all who have opportunities to influence youth? Pray *for* them, and as much as possible pray *with* them. Select a few and be like Paul: pray for them "practically all the time." Let prayers for them go out, as the NKJV translates Paul's expression, "night and day."

CERTAINTIES

I see seven absolute certainties about prayer:

1. It is part of God's plan to grant us, in answer to the prayer of faith, that which He would not give if we didn't ask (Luke 11:9, 13; James 4:3).

After two illustrations about prayer in Luke 11:5-11, Jesus declared: "If you then, being evil, know how to give good gifts to your children, how much more will your heavenly Father give the Holy Spirit to those who ask Him!" (Luke 11:13).

Here again, from chapter 4, are four absolute essentials if we expect our intercessory prayers for family and friends to make a difference:

- Faith in the blood of Jesus
- The Word in our lives and theirs
- A strong dependence on the Holy Spirit
- Appropriation of the above through fervent prayer

Without the fervent prayer the other three have less influence. That's just the way it is; God planned it that way. Satan understands this; that's why he'll let you do almost anything but pray. When we pray—really pray—he trembles and flees.

2. Prayer gives God the right to do things He otherwise could not do without interference from Satan.

Here's why: we are engaged in a great controversy, with rules of engagement on both sides. Satan, for example, cannot force anyone to sin. And God, by His very nature, will never use force, nor will He flatter or deceive. If God were to give generous amounts of the Holy Spirit before we ask, Satan would complain, "God, you have no right to do that." But when we ask, if Satan objects, God can tell him, "Be quiet; I have been *asked* to do this. So scram!" And Satan has to slink away.

3. Every prayer, if prayed in the name and in the spirit (attitude) of Christ, has an influence for good, and bears some kind of fruit (John 15:7, 8).

What we call a *petition* generally is for personal needs. *Intercession* tends to be prayers for other persons, groups, or causes. Petitions may be denied, or the answer postponed until certain conditions are met. Every unselfish intercessory prayer, however, if backed by faith in the blood of Jesus, is heard and will have an influence for good.

Both Jesus and Paul connect the word *watch* with prayer (Mark 13:33; 14:38, Colossians 4:2, KJV). Ellen White defines watch: "God will . . . answer if we watch unto prayer, if we believe we receive the things we ask for, and keep believing and never lose patience in believing. This is watching unto prayer" (*Our High Calling,* 134).

Here's further comment: "We guard the prayer of faith with expectancy and hope. We must wall it in with assurance and be not faithless, but believing. The fervent prayer of the righteous is never lost. The answer may not come according as we expected, but it will come, because God's word is pledged" (Ibid.).

4. The most important petition I can make is for personal salvation, and any time I fall into sin my first priority must be asking for forgiveness.

For salvation Jesus has promised, "The one who comes to Me I will by no means cast out (John 6:37). And here's a promise for when we sin: "If we confess our sins He is faithful and just to forgive us our sins, and to cleanse us from all unrighteousness" (1 John 1:9).

5. Whether a personal petition or intercession for others, there may be things to be made right in order for God to fully answer our prayers.

"If the wicked restores the pledge, gives back what he has stolen, and walks in the statutes of life without committing iniquity . . . none of his sins which he has committed shall be remembered against him" (Ezekiel 33:15, 16).

Space does not permit further coverage here, but the readily accessible *Steps to Christ,* in the chapter "The Privilege of Prayer," deals with this, as do my books *30 Days to a More Powerful Prayer Life* and *Whatever It Takes Praying.*

6. Answers to prayer are never earned; our only basis for expecting answers is the blood of Christ.

Any time I pray, no matter how unselfishly, Satan accuses me before God (Revelation 12:10). Like with Joshua the High Priest in Zechariah 3, I have no merit, and my goodness is like filthy rags. Then as I confess my sinfulness and claim the blood of Christ, Jesus removes the filthy rags and puts His robe of righteousness on me (verses 3, 4)

7. Every prayer backed by the blood of Christ goes into God's book of remembrance (Malachi 3:16).

"Every act of love, every word of kindness, every prayer in behalf of the suffering and oppressed, is reported before the eternal throne and placed on heaven's imperishable record" (*My Life Today,* page 237).

In 1 John, right after talking about the power of the blood of Christ to cleanse from all sin (1:7, 9), the author says: "My little children, these things I write to you so that you may not sin. And if anyone sins, we have an Advocate with the Father, Jesus Christ the righteous" (2:1).

Here's a fantastic comment on the preceding promise: "Satan stands at our right hand to accuse us, and our Advocate at God's right hand to plead for us. He has never lost a case that has been committed to Him. We may safely trust our Advocate; for He pleads His own merits in our behalf" (*Our High Calling,* page 49).

I glanced at the context when typing the preceding comment and found something else that can help increase your courage and faith as you intercede for friends, children, or whomever: "The blood of Jesus is pleading with power and efficacy for those who are backslidden, for those who are rebellious, for those who sin against great light and love" (Ibid.).

Youth, do you have any backslidden friends? Parents, any rebellious children? Pastors, any members sinning against light? Let's urge, really urge, the blood of Jesus in their behalf!

THE "SOMETHING NEW" CATEGORY

Do you remember the suggestion I shared from *My Life Today* in chapter 12? "Every day you should learn something new from the Scriptures" (page 22). The other morning I found a life-changing "something new" in this verse: "Let no corrupt word proceed out of your mouth, but what is good for necessary edification, that it may impart grace to the hearers" (Ephesians 4:29).

As with most teachers, I have at times written letters of correction. Here's what the Spirit suggested: "Never mail an already completed letter of correction until you take a couple of days to pray about its content. Make sure that it will 'impart grace' to the reader."

Here's still other applications I got for personal use from that "impart grace" phrase: (1) From now on, with every letter I mail, I will first ask God to help it impart grace to the receiver, (2) before teaching a class, I will try to remember to ask God to impart grace to every student, (3) at home I will seek to have every thing I say to my wife impart grace to her.

See what you can do with this idea. You'll come up with a lot more "impart grace" ideas.

USING SHORT PRAYERS

The other morning, I sought for a few short Bible expressions that could be turned into intercessory prayers. I wanted powerful phrases that could be used as we pray for God to raise up tens of thousands of Spirit-filled youth and adults. The Lord led me to focus on expressions with the word *filled*.

From Philippians 1:9-11 I selected *being filled with the fruits of righteousness* (verse 11). *Being filled* suggests an on-going process of being filled with "the fruits of righteousness."

The next came from the ending of Paul's prayer in Ephesians 3:14-19, namely, *filled with all the fullness of God*. At times I simply pray, "Filled, filled," as a two-word petition. Just two words, but if Spirit-empowered their impact can be immense. "Prevailing prayer," writes Wesley Duewel in *Mighty Prevailing Prayer*, "is potentially the greatest continuing threat to Satan that there has been since Calvary" (page 157).

There is also a powerful "filled" petition in this conclusion to one of David's psalms:

> Blessed be the Lord God, the God of Israel, Who only does wondrous things! And blessed be His glorious name forever! And let the whole earth be filled with His glory. Amen and Amen (Psalm 72:18, 19).

I often use the full two verses as a prayer, and at other times just these words: "Let the whole earth be filled with His glory." The following identifies Christ's glory as His character: "And the Word became flesh and dwelt among us, and we beheld His glory . . . full of grace and truth" (John 1:14). Thus, in praying "Let the whole earth be filled with His glory," I am asking that God raise up people all through "the whole earth" who will reflect the character of Christ.

FOCUSING ON APPLICATION

- *For discussion: Which of the seven certainties about prayer given in this chapter do you see as most important? Why?*

- *Here again is an assurance cited in chapter 8: "Every sincere prayer that is offered is mingled with the efficacy of Christ's blood. If the answer is deferred, it is because God desires us to show a holy boldness in claiming the pledged word of God" (In Heavenly Places, page 74). Why not put that on a 3-by-5 card? Then use it as a faith-builder as you plead the blood of Christ in behalf of youth or other special people on your prayer list.*

You might also try using "filled" or "being filled" as a one or two word petition. Or use "Let the whole earth be filled with His glory." Even short prayers, if "mingled with the efficacy of Christ's blood," make a difference.

Chapter 15

A Passion to Pray Without Ceasing

"Rejoice always.
Pray without ceasing."
(1 Thessalonians 5:16, 17)

The time: April of 1996.

The place: Spring Valley Academy, near Kettering, Ohio. The occasion: A senior, Delinda Snyder, in tears because at that time large numbers of her fellow students seemed indifferent to the claims of Christ.

Hazel Burns, associate pastor at the Kettering Adventist Church, had been going to the academy to pray with Delinda and a few others. Of this day Delinda later said, "As I prayed about my burden for my school, my praying became intense. I couldn't hold back the tears."

At that time a prayer conference in England was only two weeks away.

Spring Valley would be sending seven students. Because Delinda was a senior, she was not eligible to go; the school wanted only those who would be back to influence the 1996–97 school.

After Delinda and Mrs. Burns had prayed, Hazel told her, "Delinda, you're going to England,"

"But I can't," Delinda said. "I'm a senior, I don't have $2,000 for the trip, and it's almost too late to get a passport."

"I'm going to pray about this," Hazel said.

The next morning Hazel went to the academy to see Delinda. "When I got to the office this morning," she said, "I knelt to pray. I had barely started when there was a knock on the door." When she answered, Cheryl, a person she had led to the Lord, said to her, "Hazel, I want to donate $2,000 for however you want to use it."

Ninety youth went, mostly from the Dakotas, California, and Ohio. "When we got there we were to spend a week in training," Delinda said, "and then a week doing prayer conferences, and helping wherever the pastors of the South England Conference wanted us."

Many things did not go as planned. "That," Delinda said, "put us out of our comfort zone." But later, looking back, she said, "We learned to trust in God, and He never failed us."

"WHAT HAPPENED TO YOU?"

Many young lives were touched. When the seven from Spring Valley Academy got back, other students began to ask, "What happened to you? You're different."

"Come to the church Friday evening and we will tell you," said Greg Taylor, a junior at the academy.

A dozen came. Within three weeks sixty youth were meeting together to pray and study the Bible. "Things changed on our campus," said Delinda. "You would see students praying together in halls and classrooms. It became natural to talk about Christ."

In June both Delinda and Greg, and two youth from California, helped with youth meetings at the Dakota camp meeting. I met them there, and shortly afterwards sent a questionnaire about their experience. Here, in condensed form, are Delinda and Greg's replies:

1. What were your private prayer habits like before attending the England prayer conference?

Delinda: "I prayed before every meal, at bedtime, and sometimes before a test."

Greg: "I didn't realize it but I had been praying less and less."

2. What changes, if any, did the conference make in your private prayer habits?

Delinda: "I now pray continually—literally all day long."

Greg: "I started to pray from the heart. I began not only asking for things, but praising God. Prayer became more real."

3. What were your Bible reading habits like before attending the conference?

Delinda: "I tried to read a section of the Bible every morning, but didn't always do it."

Greg: "I had read the Bible every evening. I usually hoped the next chapter would be short, so I could get to bed earlier."

4. What changes, if any, did the conference make in your Bible study habits?

Delinda: "I started reading a section and then studying it for as long as three days."

Greg: "I saw a meaning in texts that I had never seen. Bible study became very important."

5. What changes did the conference make in your interest in praying with others, as in a small group?

Delinda: "I feel totally comfortable now praying in a large group. I know I don't have to say anything fancy, just what is on my heart."

Greg: "I started making friends with people that I never would have before. We are becoming united under God."

6. What did you enjoy most in that first prayer conference?

Delinda: "I loved seeing God's power! So many times we expect God to follow *our* plan and that is not what He has in mind. We then think God has failed us when really He has a better plan."

Greg: "It was so cool seeing kids our age excited about God, and motivated to know Him."

7. Back home how have you used the skills and ideas you gained?

Delinda: "We started a Friday night Bible study at which the first night we had only ten people but which in three weeks we had sixty people. As a result of the studies, we have had four baptisms. Our school has been totally turned around."

Greg: "I helped start our Friday night Bible study, and through God I have been given strength to talk to my friends about God. One of them is now on fire about God. I have also shared in church what God has done for me."

8. Please write a short testimony about your experience.

Delinda: "That will be difficult; I would need heavenly words to tell what I gained in England! I learned that God is not like what I had thought, and my faith was stretched beyond what I had thought it could be stretched. Everything comfortable was taken away from me and it was only then that I had complete trust and faith in God. Amazing things happen when we just trust."

Greg: "In England I found courage and strength. I had friends who meant a lot to me, but our focus was not God. While in England my life changed. God became my reason for living, and I thought, 'I've got to share this with my friends.' Then fear struck. I told myself, They won't listen; they'll think I'm weird. Then I faced the fact that if I talked abut my love for God I might lose a friend, but if I don't I might lose an eternal friend.

"So I prayed and God strengthened me and I talked to them. At first they laughed, but later they realized I wasn't joking. My best friend, Chad, began to love God and became my friend for life, literally for eternity. I thank God for giving me the courage to share with him."

PRAYING WITHOUT CEASING

Paul urged, "Pray without ceasing" (1 Thessalonians 5: 17). "I now pray continually," Delinda wrote.

Is that possible? It *is.* All God's commands contain implied promises. In reality God says, "I will help you to pray without ceasing." But how? The usual answer is this: Try to maintain a prayerful attitude. I sometimes refer to a suggestion in *Messages to Young People* that while engaged in our daily work, we should lift the soul to heaven in prayer, and that this baffles Satan (page 249).

It was thus that Enoch "walked with God" (Genesis 5:24). But in the context I found something else—a truth about prayer that opens up incredible possibilities. It's this:

When engaged in our daily labor, we may breathe out our heart's desire, inaudible to any human ear; but that word cannot die away into silence, nor can it be lost. Nothing can drown the soul's desire. It rises above the din of the street, above the noise of machinery. It is God to whom we are speaking, and our prayer is heard (page 250).

Do you see what that means? Every Christlike "heart's desire" God sees as a prayer! Here's what I've concluded: *Every such desire makes a difference!* In chapter 2 I mentioned that I have been praying that by the year 2001 God will raise up 100,000 Spirit-filled youth, wholly committed, artesian wells of love, and determined to live by every word that comes from God. It has become a passion with me that is almost continually in my thoughts.

APPLICATIONS

Here's another idea to test: The little book *Thoughts From the Mount of Blessing* suggests, "Every promise in the word of God furnishes us with subject matter for prayer" (page 133). Perhaps that could be said for ideas from the varied Ellen White books and others.

Paul preceded his suggestion, "Pray without ceasing," with "Rejoice evermore" (1 Thessalonians 5:16, KJV). I think you'll find that on those days when you fill the day with many silent "Thank Yous" to God, it will be easier to maintain a spirit of prayer. Currently I'm trying to develop the habit of a "Thank You" to God every time I get a drink of water—both for the water and for the symbolism of water representing the Holy Spirit.

Even when things go wrong, I'm trying to silently praise God (and learn from the problem when it's my own fault). *Steps to Christ* points out that our heavenly Father takes "an immediate interest" in our every joy, our every perplexity, and every calamity (page 100).

Will you join me in cultivating godly desires for the salvation of the youth, friends, and others of your acquaintance? Here are other options to test:

- *Train yourself to recognize every godly desire as a prayer. Remember that such desires cannot "die away into silence." Every such desire is heard.*
- *Review chapter 2 and join me and thousands of others in earnest prayer to God that He will raise up an army of Spirit-filled youth by the start of the year 2001. And, along with these, an army of leaders and laymen in the Adventist Church who are totally surrendered and Spirit-filled.*
- *Try making Bible verses or passages content for prayer. At times you may want to write a Bible verse or short passage on a 3-by-5 card to keep with you during the day. Then when you have a moment for silent prayer—waiting in line, while driving, etc.—use the thoughts on the card as "subject matter for prayer."*

Chapter 16

A Passion for Purity in Christ

"Happy are those whose greatest desire is to do what God requires;
God will satisfy them fully! . . . Happy are the pure in heart;
they will see God!"
(Matthew 5:6, 8, Today's English Version)

"When I got married I was three months pregnant," a girl attending a wedding reception said with tears in her eyes. "I had no choice. I cried through the whole wedding. It was the saddest day of my life."

As the above two Beatitudes bring out, it doesn't need to be that way. Last Christmas (1997) one of our prayer conference student leaders gave me a copy of Max Lucado's *God's Inspirational Promise Book*. On the last page of the book Lucado asks, "What is more beautiful than a bride?"

"Maybe it is the aura of whiteness that clings to her as dew clings to a rose. Or perhaps it is the diamonds that glisten in her eyes. Or maybe it's the blush of love that pinks her cheeks or the bouquet of promises she carries" (page 201).

It made me think of my own bride when we were married in the church at Union College. I love Lucado's next paragraph: "A bride. A commitment robed in elegance. 'I'll be with you forever.' Tomorrow bringing hope today. Promised purity faithfully delivered."

Promised purity faithfully delivered. In my own marriage, neither of us had had previous sexual involvement. The first night was "promised purity faithfully delivered." What God intended in Genesis 2—"they shall become one flesh"—is truly one of the great blessings of marriage.

To encourage them to develop the habit of early morning devotions, I ask my Workshop in Prayer students to daily read from the devotional book *In Heavenly Places.* Months read include July: first about the body as a temple, then about marriage and family.

The Bible text for July 14 is: "He who finds a wife finds a good thing, And obtains favor from the Lord" (Proverbs 18:22). The reverse, of course, is equally true. Here's a sentence from the July 14 comments: "Marriage, when joined with purity and holiness, truth and righteousness, is one of the greatest blessings ever given to the human family" (page 202).

I can only say, Amen and Amen!

FROM THE WORST, THE BEST

An article in *Time,* June 1998, was titled "Where'd You Learn That?" It had a subtitle that read, "American kids are in the midst of their own sexual revolution."

It's not just kids and teens, however. A year earlier the front cover of *US News & World Report* (5/19/97) featured an article titled "The Trouble With Premarital Sex." The six-page article pointed out that many more people in their 20s give birth to babies out of wedlock than do teens.

The fact that half of marriages today end in divorce is strong evidence that today's preoccupation with sex has not brought the kind of happiness the two Beatitudes at the start of this chapter describe.

Yet out of the worst, God intends to bring the best—a final generation of believers who will reflect His purity more completely than any other.

No one of any age, married or unmarried, is immune to sexual temptation. The May 15, 1997, issue of *The Adventist Review* had an article titled "The Psychology of an Affair." The author, a retired pastor in Phoenix, Arizona, tells of the exercise "high" he gets from climbing a peak in Phoenix—at the top, that is.

On the way down he sometimes gets another high—a social one from hikers with whom he descends. He says, "Let me be quite honest. Even at seventy, if I'm talking and walking with a young woman with blue eyes, fair hair, and a Barbie doll figure, the high is even greater."

He writes that two people of opposite sex in a recreational or work situation, even if both have a spouse, can "generate a natural attraction" like a drug high. If fantasy and inappropriate association are not guarded against, an affair often develops.

DEALING WITH TEMPTATION

What's the best way to handle pre-marital and extra-marital sexual temptations? Consider these suggestions:

1. Let's all seek to live this statement from Christ's John 17 prayer: "For their sakes I sanctify Myself" (John 17:19).

Almost all of us—whether unmarried, engaged, happily married, or divorced—encounter moments of ungodly sexual desires. During those times we can look on the people who are sexual temptations the way Christ looked on those He prayed for in John 17. We can see them as they might become through our prayers and influence, if godly, and declare, "*For their sakes* I will seek the sanctification God offers through my study of His Word."

For me this has become one of the strongest reasons to subdue impulses toward an out-of-marriage sexual attraction.

2. If we find ourselves being sexually attracted to someone to whom we have no right, we do well to form the habit seeing that person as clothed with the righteousness of Christ.

In the Laodicean message Jesus calls that righteousness "white garments" (Revelation 3:18). Men can view all women, whether a follower of Jesus or not, as potentially clothed with those "white garments." This can work even if she is a bikini-clad bather on a beach.

If you are a married woman and you are attracted toward a male with a good physique who isn't your husband, try this: Picture that handsome guy as clothed with the "white garments" Christ offers all men. Even if he apparently isn't thus clothed, in your mind's eye picture him that way. It should help restrain unlawful desires.

3. For the married, Proverbs 5 suggests this safeguard against out-of-marriage affairs: become and remain "enraptured" with your spouse.

Titled "The Peril of Adultery" or "Warning Against Immorality" in the

NKJV, Proverbs 5 is directed to men. In today's society, however, its suggestions are equally effective for helping women to avoid affairs. The basic principle is this: "Drink water from your own cistern, and running water from your own well" (verse 15). The author makes his meaning clear by adding:

> Let your fountain be blessed, and rejoice with the wife of your youth. As a loving deer and a graceful doe, let her breasts satisfy you at all times; and always be enraptured with her love. For why should you, my son, be enraptured by an immoral woman? (verses 18-20).

I checked the wording of the above passage in many versions. Here are some of the ways the word "enraptured" has been translated: "infatuated" (RSV), "ravished" (KJV), "be ravished" (Moffatt), and "continually ravished" (AAT).

Whether husband or wife, anyone who cultivates that kind of experience with his or her spouse is unlikely to develop an affair!

4. *Try using the following prayer, and repeat it both for yourself and for anyone who may be a sexual temptation:*

> Save me in spite of myself; my weak, unchristlike self. Lord, take my heart [or our hearts], for I [we] cannot give it [them]. It is Thy property. Keep it pure, for I cannot keep it for Thee. Mold me, fashion me, raise me into a pure and holy atmosphere, where the rich current of Thy love can flow through my soul (*Christ's Object Lessons*, page 159).

The above is a paraphrase of the publican's prayer, "God, be merciful to me a sinner!" (Luke 18:13). I first wrote it on a 3-by-5 card and used it for myself until I had it memorized.

One Friday evening I presented a Bible study worship for about fifteen students at Andrews, and gave them a handout with three of Paul's prayers and the above on it. To conclude we divided into groups of four to pray. One girl in my group included the above by reading it as part of her prayer, and afterwards thanked me for it.

To my amazement, three other college girls spoke to me about what a blessing it was to get a handout that included the *Christ's Object Lessons* prayer.

In moments of temptation you may need to pray it more than once, but I have learned that whatever the temptation, silently praying it brings to my side the One who has promised, "I am with you always" (Matthew 28:20). The

Holy Spirit goes to work, and He quietly dissolves the sexual temptation.

5. For me there's still another truth that helps: look on every young woman or young man as a sacred temple to be filled by the Holy Spirit.

Between 1 Corinthians 6:9 and 10:31 Paul repeatedly mentions things that have to do with sexual purity and/or marriage and its sexual privileges. The basis for everything he says is this statement:

> Don't you know that your body is the temple of the Holy Spirit, who lives in you and who was given to you by God? You do not belong to yourselves but to God; he bought you for a price. So use your bodies for God's glory (1 Corinthians 6:19, 20, TEV).

"In sexual sin we violate the sacredness of our own bodies," is the way *The Message* paraphrases the last part of the verse that precedes the above.

As you meet people, along with a greeting think of that person as a sacred temple, and silently breathe these words from Paul as a prayer: God make you a sacred temple.

IDEAS TO TEST

- *After he mentioned fornicators, adulterers, homosexuals, and sodomites in 1 Corinthians 6, Paul said, "Such were some of you, but you were washed, but you were sanctified, but you were justified in the name of the Lord Jesus and by the Spirit of our God" (verses 9-11). What hope does this offer for the girl mentioned in the first paragraph of this chapter?*
- *Review the five suggestions for dealing with sexual temptations. Which one or ones do you see as most helpful for unmarried or divorced people? Which one or ones for married people?*
- *Try writing the prayer from* Christ's Object Lessons *on a 3-by-5 card. If you are a student, begin to use it for yourself and fellow students by changing the pronouns to make the wording inclusive.*
- *If an older person, use the same prayer for Christian youth everywhere. And don't forget to include yourself.*

Chapter 17

Blessings From Reconciliation

"I do not pray for these alone, but also for those who will believe in me through their word; that they all may be one, as You are in Me, and I in You, that they may also be one in Us, that the world may believe that You sent Me."
(John 17:20, 21)

What do you see as the worst kind of emotional pain?

Probably most people would say there's nothing worse than the loss of a loved one in death. A close second is barriers that separate a husband and wife from each other.

My wife and I recently got new insights about that pain. In a camp meeting setting, we ate several times with a former student whose wife has filed for divorce. He loves her very much, but she has cut all communication with him for someone else. The anguish and pain that kind of situation inflicts is terrible.

As my wife and I prayed for and with him, it dawned on me that our heavenly Father lives with that kind of pain day and night. Untold numbers of people who once lived close to God and talked with Him freely have cut off all communication with their Lord. Their Father loves them intensely, yet they seek total separation from Him. And not just one, but hundreds and thousands. Can we even imagine the kind of pain that inflicts on God?

That realization makes me love my heavenly Father more than ever! In praying for others it also motivates me to want to enter into His feelings. As I have tried to do so, God has become more and more precious. It has given me a passion greater than ever before to develop an ever closer relationship with Him. I don't want anything in my life to inflict pain on Him.

REACHING OUT IN FAITH

This afternoon I spent an hour doing some yardwork. As I thought of finishing this manuscript, I simply said one word, "Father." Then as my mind went to my wife, and to various students, again, just a one-word prayer, "Father."

This July morning during private devotions I had spent time with Paul's prayer in Colossians 1:9-14 for the church members there. Several times I have written in this book about the blood of Jesus, as shed on Calvary. When praying for Adventist youth, at times I mention that blood to God in prayers like this:

> Dear Father, in Colossians 1 Paul ends his prayer by speaking of the blood of Christ—that 'we have redemption through His blood, and forgiveness of sins' (verse 14). I claim that blood in behalf of all 81 Adventist colleges and universities, all 930 academies, and all 4,500 elementary schools, and all Adventist youth in public schools. Let Christ's blood be placed upon the doorpost of every mind on those campuses this summer, and on all who will be returning to campus this fall.

After time in Colossians, I remembered that the scourging and crucifixion of Jesus are not the first mention of His blood. I turned to Luke 22 and read the story of Christ sweating blood as He prayed in Gethsemane (Luke 22:39-46). "And being in agony, He prayed more earnestly. Then His sweat became like great drops of blood falling down to the ground" (verse 44).

"I've overlooked that reference as a basis for intercessory prayer," I told myself. For the rest of the day, in praying for youth I used these words as thought prayers: *Father. The blood in Gethsemane.* Over and over again, *Father. The blood in Gethsemane.* Then on a short evening walk, *Father. The blood in Gethsemane.*

When it comes to reconciliation—in families, in congregations, or wherever, no argument is more powerful than an appeal by us to Christ's blood. We could be urging the blood of Christ when we pray about the differences among us as families and as congregations.

Let's go to a story about reconciliation.

THE DIFFERENCE FAITH MAKES

I began pastoring the Coloma church in 1990, and the next summer the Michigan Conference paid two undergraduate students at Andrews to spend several weeks doing visitation and then holding three weeks of evangelistic meetings. The church raised funds to also hire two young women from Andrews.

In looking for Bible studies, one team knocked on the door at a trailer house several miles into the country. When they asked Sherrie Koshar, the young wife who came to the door if she would like to study the Bible with them, Sherrie replied, "Just last night I prayed to God to help me understand the Bible." Monte and Gazelle, the two students, began studies with her and with her husband Pete. They didn't attend the meetings, but during the following school year they continued the studies.

From almost its beginning, Pete and Sherrie's marriage had been rocky. As an illustration of the difference Christ, prayer, and Bible study can make in a marriage, I asked Sherrie to write out a testimony about their experience:

I was a senior in high school when I started dating Pete. We had a roller coaster relationship—breaking up, getting back together, breaking up again, etc.—before we married and had a baby. Up until the time our son was around three, we went to church on Sunday, to family activities, and appeared to have an average family.

I say "appeared" because we had lots of problems. Pete has many wonderful qualities, but he would get drunk, and I'd get angry and complain. More drunkenness, more complaining. I didn't like the person I was becoming. One night, after a hard episode, Pete went out as usual. As usual, I felt lonely and disappointed. As usual, I worried about Pete's safety.

I knew our marriage was crumbling. I felt I had no option except to file for divorce. In tears I flung myself on the bed. I saw myself as becoming mean, ungrateful.

Alone, I began to pray. I hurt for our son. I didn't know if I should try to hang on in a drinking environment or get out. I prayed most of the night, only to be startled by the ringing of the phone. Pete had again been picked up for drunk driving and was in jail.

Pete spent three months in jail. I kept praying for wisdom and strength. When Pete was released and came home, our son feared him. That helped Pete realize he needed to stop drinking. He also realized he had to choose between drinking and jail, or no alcohol and staying out of jail.

He quit, but other problems remained. Ten years before this I had purchased Bible Story books, and one day two Andrews University students named Monte and Gazelle came to our trailer. They asked if I would like to study the Bible with them.

I insisted that Pete stay for the study . . . and he did! From that point on we studied with Monte and Gazelle for about a year. I thought things were looking up. I was shocked when Pete told me he was leaving me. Alcohol had been out of our lives for a year, so I couldn't blame that.

Again, I lay in my room praying with all my heart. I didn't know what to do. I didn't want to pretend for our son. I didn't want to be a failure. I prayed for strength and guidance to do God's will, and gave everything to Him, put the whole mess in the Lord's hand. What a burden that lifted from my heart.

The next morning Pete did leave home, but he returned that evening. For the next two months we lived in the same house but didn't really speak to each other.

I kept praying.

Then things began to change. We attended a Revelation Seminar at the Coloma church and started keeping the Sabbath, and eventually Pastor Joe baptized me, and some months later Pete was baptized.

Our marriage has grown. I can't even imagine being without my husband now. If fact, in some ways I wish I could be more like him. We've since had another son. The Lord lives in our home and in all of our hearts.

I continue to thank God for loving me and giving me a WONDERFUL life. I thank Him for teaching me how to pray. I've learned how to pray with my heart without using words. What a blessing!

As I wrote this testimony, there were times I stopped to cry as I recalled certain feelings and emotions. I asked for courage, strength, and guidance, and He gave them to me. I thank Him for bringing us where we are today. He is our best Friend and He is always there.

LOOKING FOR USABLE IDEAS

Families aren't the only place where a healing touch is needed. Far too many churches have factions and differences between members.

After the ascension of Jesus, a lot of strong feelings separated the disciples. It was only after they had become reconciled that God was able to pour out His Spirit. Could it be that the biggest reason that God has not given the latter rain is because of differences in our families and in our churches?

- *The prayer of Jesus in John 17 can be divided into three parts: first for Himself (1-5), then for His family, the disciples (6-19), then for all future believers, including us (20-26). What do you see as methods that help families and church congregations to truly become one?*
- *Spend some time with Paul's prayer in Colossians 1:9-14. Then consider incorporating some of its ideas into your prayers for unity in families and churches.*
- *What one idea in this chapter made the deepest impression on you?*

Chapter 18

A Passion for Fitness

*"Whether you eat or drink, or whatever you do,
do all to the glory of God."*
(1 Corinthians 10:31)

Take care of your health—"there's only one body per customer."

That's the advice of Grandma Whitney, the woman who first climbed Mt. Whitney when she was sixty-six, and who at age ninety-one made her twenty-third and final trip to the top of the highest peak in the continental United States. (Six weeks before that she had climbed Mt. Fuji in Japan).

About fifteen years ago Hulda Crooks, the grandma of the book *Grandma Whitney: Queen of the Mountain*, spent a few days in Berrien Springs, and I arranged for her to visit my Workshop in Prayer class. She told some of her mountain climbing experiences, took questions, and encouraged my students to eat right, get adequate sleep, and get exercise.

In this chapter I interview Dan Snyder. He and his sister Delinda are setting a few records of their own in mountain climbing and in the process are keeping in excellent physical shape. Dan graduated from Andrews University in 1998 with a degree in aviation and currently teaches flying there. Delinda is a junior at Andrews, majoring in theology.

Right after graduation Dan, Delinda, their father Terry Snyder, and seven friends made a six-day climb from Jackson Hole, Wyoming, up around and behind the three Grand Tetons Peaks, using snowshoes in the upper elevations. I asked Dan a few questions about their experiences, and about keeping at one's best physically.

Pastor Joe: Dan, what are some of the climbs you and your sister have made during the last year and half?

Dan: The Adirondacks during Christmas break in 1996, Mt. Whitney during spring break of 1997, the Tetons at the close of school in June of '97, Mt. Washington during the Christmas break of '97, and the Tetons again last month.

Pastor Joe: I've taken students up Mt. Whitney a couple of times, but always over Labor Day. What's it like in March?

Dan: A lot of snow. Before we reached the summit it was six feet deep. In the snow we wore shoes with crampons. The first day we climbed to Mirror Lake, at 10,000 feet, slept there, and went to the top the next day, then back to Mirror Lake and to our cars at Whitney Portals.

Pastor Joe: What do you see from on top?

Dan: To the east you look down on Death Valley. To the north, south, and west, you see a lot of other peaks that are 14,000 feet or higher.

Pastor Joe: Shortly after your Whitney climb your sister gave a talk at a prayer conference at the Worthington, Ohio church. I still remember an illustration she used: You reach the top one step at a time. Keep your eyes fixed on Jesus, and keep climbing. With Him you'll make it.

I've heard Mt. Washington in New Hampshire gets bitterly cold, with winds up to 100 miles an hour. What was it like last December?

Dan: At the start the temperature was about 25 degrees. The second night we had seventy miles per hour winds, with a wind chill of minus 20. The next day the wind chill dropped to minus 40. We slept on top New Year's Eve. The wind chill was minus 80.

Pastor Joe: Why do you punish yourself with that kind of extreme cold?

Dan: With down bags we keep warm. We like challenges; climbing mountains gives one a healthful challenge.

Pastor Joe: And the Grand Canyon? You've also been in and out of it. What's that trip like?

Dan: We went down from the South Rim, taking the Bright Angel Trail down to the Colorado River. The elevation drops almost a mile, which makes coming out the climb.

Pastor Joe: What do you most remember about that trip?

Dan: It was hot! We were there in June, and it was also humid, especially at the bottom. But you don't swim; the water comes out of the dam upriver, at about fifty degrees.

Pastor Joe: How old were you and Delinda when you first started climbing?

Dan: Our first high climb was in 1985, Long's Peak in Colorado, when I was eleven and Delinda nine. We first backpacked with our parents in the Smokies when I was a little over five and Delinda a little over three.

Pastor Joe: Dan, to what do you attribute you and your sister's keen interest in physical fitness?

Dan: Necessity. We got a love of the outdoors from our parents, who were doing a lot of hiking. For the kind of trips we take, we've got to keep in shape.

Pastor Joe: What do you see as the basics for staying in shape?

Dan: Four things: Adequate sleep, eating right, exercise, and a healthy mind set.

KEEPING FIT

Most of us don't have opportunity to climb mountains, but we can build into our lifestyle the four basics Dan mentioned. Let's start with adequate sleep. In my Workshop on Prayer class I often have students memorize this sentence from the book *Education:*

> Since the work of building up the body takes place during the hours of rest, it is essential, especially in youth, that sleep should be regular and abundant (page 205).

I emphasize two words: *regular* and *abundant.* College and academy students often don't get either; reasons include taking an overload, procrastination, poor planning, television, and other forms of wasted time. Many adults also attempt too much, and multitudes hurt themselves both physically and spiritually with late TV shows.

In Adventist education, the book *Counsels to Parents, Teachers, and Students* (it's for students too!) recommends that "in our schools the lights should be put out at half past nine" (page 297). Students "will then rise refreshed for the duties of the day" (Ibid.). Like a lot of other things that *Counsels to Teachers* and *Education* urge, most of us have gotten away from that advice.

Solomon spoke of a sleep that is "sweet" because of physical labor (Ecclesiastes 5:12). Here's a repeat (from chapter 8) of something that was shown Ellen White about sleep:

> I know from the testimonies given me from time to time for brain workers, that sleep is worth far more before than after midnight. Two hours good sleep before twelve o'clock is worth more than four hours after twelve o'clock (see *7 Manuscript Releases*, page *224*).

The word "good" implies enough physical weariness to rest well. And the "given from time to time" must be some indication of the importance of the advice. We pray, "Thy will be done." Do we really mean what we pray when it comes to forming good habits? Where are those who seek to live by the "every word" Jesus urged in Matthew 4:4?

EATING RIGHT

In 1900 heart disease caused just under 8 percent of the deaths in the United States. Today in America cardiovascular disease causes 50 percent of the deaths. A similar increase in deaths from heart disease has also been seen in other parts of the Western World.

Why? It's largely because of what we eat, and a lack of exercise.

First, the hazards from a lot of junk food—big amounts of fats and sugars in particular. Many of us get up to 40 percent of our calories from fat, which helps put cholesterol levels above 200.

In his book *To Your Health*, Hans Diehl suggests that those who keep their cholesterol level down to 150 or less are almost certain to never have a heart attack. To keep it down, he recommends that we cut fat intake to 10 percent of our caloric intake.

"The 10 percent solution"—that was the headline in the September 28, 1992, issue of the South Bend *Tribune*. A subheading read, "If Americans could limit fat consumption to a tenth of their total calories, 'heart disease could be as rare as polio or malaria,' one doctor says" (D1).

In Adventist schools, most food services use cheese and a lot of high fat preparations because that's what students' taste buds demand. I eat at the Andrews cafeteria quite often, and notice that only a small number leave off cheese and similar fat-filled foods. What would it take to bring some changes?

EXERCISE

In one list of the most dangerous occupations, the top five are: the manufacture and storage of explosives, coal-mining, logging, using power saws and other power tools, and exposure to radioactive substances. From another Adventist book about education—*Fundamentals of Christian Education*—here's another perspective:

> The occupations requiring sedentary habits are the most dangerous for they take men away from the open air and sunshine, and train one set of faculties while other organs are becoming weak from inaction. Men carry on their work, perfect their business, and soon lie down in the grave (page 319).

A century ago, when that was written, an estimated 50 percent of the work force got sufficient exercise on the job. And today? About 2 percent.

Perfect health requires perfect circulation. An active muscle has up to ten times as much blood flowing through it as an inactive muscle. We can't do much about the fact that jobs today are largely sedentary, but most of us can do a lot more walking—the best of all kinds of exercise.

A HEALTHY MIND-SET

Moderate exercise also helps lay a foundation for a healthy mind. An improved flow of blood helps dispel depressed, melancholy feelings.

The religion of Christ does much toward developing a healthy mind-set. The wisdom that leads one to choose Christ brings "length of days" and "pleasantness" and "peace" (Proverbs 3:13-18).

Here's a striking comment from *My Life Today*:

> Sickness of the mind prevails everywhere. Nine tenths of the diseases from which men suffer have their foundations here. . . . The religion of

Christ . . . is one of the most effectual remedies, for it is a potent soother of the nerves (page 149).

At a time when a desire to be like all the nations had almost ruined Israel, God led Samuel to establish the schools of the prophets. The book *Patriarchs and Prophets* contains a chapter titled "The Schools of the Prophets." A paragraph on page 600 lists eight benefits the religion of Christ brings. Here are just four of the eight. Note how all relate to a healthy mind-set:

- Brings man into harmony with the laws of God, physical, mental, and moral
- Teaches self-control, serenity, temperance
- Ennobles the mind, refines the taste, sanctifies the judgment
- Makes the soul a partaker of the purity of heaven

What blessings!

LOTS OF OPTIONS!

As you pray about the content of this chapter, you have many options for more and still more in the way of physical, mental, and spiritual improvement. Here are a few samples:

- *What changes might you need to make in order to enjoy maximum physical health? And what changes for maximum mental health?*
- *Genesis 3 tells of Eve disobeying God on a small thing— she ate something God had forbidden. Count the numbers of time the word eat or one of its derivatives is found in Genesis 3. Then ask yourself, "What would it take for me to gain the victory over an inclination to eat things I shouldn't?"*
- *Proverbs 3:13-18 summarizes benefits from choosing wisdom. Take a little time with this passage for meditation and prayer.*
- *If you have access to a copy of* Patriarchs and Prophets, *read the chapter titled "The Schools of the Prophets." Then discuss with a family member or friend the last paragraph on page 600, where all eight benefits found in the religion of Christ are summarized.*

Chapter 19

A Passion for True Beauty

*"They looked to Him, and were radiant,
and their faces were not ashamed."*
(Psalm 34:5)

A wrinkled old woman selling cosmetics approached six beautiful girls. As she talked with them she said, "Twenty years ago I was just as beautiful as you are."

This shocked the girls so much that they vowed to never let themselves deteriorate the way the cosmetics seller had. To seal their pledge they agreed to meet exactly twenty years later to prove their point.

At the agreed upon year and day, Kathern Lambert, one of the six, went to the restaurant specified. None of the others showed up. One had committed suicide in a Paris hotel only four years after their pledge. Another, after ruining her health with extreme dieting, died in Hollywood at age thirty-four. A third died in a fire when a cigarette set her evening gown ablaze. The fourth was killed in a nightclub brawl. The fifth died penniless, an addict to drugs.

All had achieved worldly success. One had become known as "the best dressed woman on the screen." Another was the lead in a popular play. A third had married a millionaire. But all, leaving God out, had lost what beauty they had (Kenneth Wood, *Meditations for Moderns*, Review and Herald, 1963, page 320).

GROWING TOWARD BEAUTY

While doing research for this chapter, I went to the *Index to the Writings of Ellen G. White*. To my amazement, I found more that two pages of references under "Face(s)"—a total of some four hundred entries. Here's a sample about the radiance Christ adds to the facial expression:

> By the life we live through the grace of Christ . . . the original loveliness begins to be restored in the soul. The attributes of the character of Christ are imparted. . . . The faces of men and women who walk and work with God express the peace of heaven (*The Desire of Ages*, page 312).

In Romans 12:2 Paul speaks of being "transformed by the renewing of your mind." The devotional book *My Life Today*, in a comment on Paul's statement, suggests that the development of Christian character "is a growth toward beauty," and adds: "As the heart becomes transformed by the renewing of the mind, the graces of the Spirit leave their impress on the face, and it expresses the refinement, delicacy, peace, benevolence, and pure and tender love that reigns in the heart" (page 153).

Living for Christ *is a growth toward beauty!* What an encouragement for the vast majority of young women who consider themselves to be plain! Developing beauty within makes the outward features more lovely!

In her *The Official 1993 Devotional Book* Renee Kempf Coffee shared this: "Mrs. Robbins was a counselor at the high school where I used to teach. The first time we met, all I noticed were her birthmarks. Her entire face was covered with bright-red splotches. But by the end of the year they seemed to have disappeared. As I got to know her, all I saw was her beautiful personality" (page 225).

Here's an insight for men: *Steps to Christ* mentions that the face of Christ did not wear expressions of gloom "but ever one of peaceful serenity. His heart was a wellspring of life; and wherever He went He carried rest and peace, joy and gladness" (page 120).

In His followers, the author adds, levity will be repressed, with no boister-ous merriment or rude jesting. "But the religion of Jesus gives peace like a river. It does not quench the light of joy; it does not restrain cheerfulness, nor cloud the sunny, smiling face" (page 121).

WHAT A PERSON WEARS

As young people it often is not easy to shun ungodly customs and styles. Peer pressure causes many to abandon Bible teachings that have to do with dress and modesty. Usually it happens little by little; a little nail polish, a little paint on the lips, low-cut dresses, skirts above the knees, shorts that come nowhere near the knees, and with fellows jeans so loose they almost fall off.

The Bible has a surprisingly large number of references to what one wears. Equally surprising, much of it has to do with being more attractive. A basic principle is simplicity and natural beauty. Consider an example from the book of Revelation, where a church is symbolized by a woman. In Revelation 12 God used a woman dressed simply—clothed with the sun, a symbol of Christlikeness—to symbolize the true church. Note the contrast in the way the woman who represents a false church is described: "The woman was arrayed in purple and scarlet, and adorned with gold and precious stones and pearls, having in her hand a golden cup full of abominations and the filthiness of her fornication" (Revelation 17:4).

Note the positive way Paul describes the way a woman should dress and how he includes men:

I desire that in every place men should pray, lifting holy hands with-out anger or quarreling, also that women should adorn themselves modestly and sensibly in seemly apparel, not with braided hair [Phillips: elaborate coiffure] or gold or pearls or costly attire but by good deeds (1 Timothy 2:8-10, RSV).

Consider the three qualities that should characterize a woman's dress: mod-est, sensible, seemly. My dictionary defines seemly as "pleasing in appearance, fair, handsome," and as "suitable, proper, fitting, or becoming."

Good qualities for men and women alike, wouldn't you say?

THE BIBLE AND JEWELRY

If you are new to the Seventh-day Adventist Church, did it trouble you to learn that most church members do not wear jewelry, and many don't wear even a wedding band?

The Old Testament sometimes mentions God's people using jewelry—as when Eliezer presented Rebekah with "a golden nose ring weighing half a shekel, and two bracelets for her wrists weighing ten shekels of gold" (Genesis 24:22). But when people had fallen into sin, as with Jacob's family, the patriarch took "all their earrings which were in their ears" and got rid of them (see Genesis 35:2-4).

When the women of Isaiah's time became infatuated with ornaments, Isaiah saw their jewels and finery as evidence of proud, self-centered hearts. He rebuked their pride with one of the most blistering condemnations in Scripture (Isaiah 3:16-26).

In several areas of lifestyle—jewelry, multiple wives, divorce—the New Testament holds up a higher standard than the Old. The example of Christ, "I do not seek My own glory" (John 8:50), keynotes the lifestyle of the New Testament.

Ellen White lifted up the example of Jesus—His stepping down from His throne, clothing His divinity with humanity, becoming poor so that we might become rich. In that context she said this: "Those who have bracelets, and wear gold and ornaments, had better take these idols from their persons and sell them, even if it should be for much less than they gave for them, and thus practice self-denial" (*Selected Messages*, book 3, page 248).

She then pointed to the source of our problem: "Self, self, self, must be served and glorified" (Ibid.).

The wedding ring is generally disapproved because of the preceding passage by Paul asking that gold and pearls not be worn. Peter says something similar in 1 Peter 3:3, 4.

THE BODY AS A TEMPLE

As you study and pray about what the Bible teaches on topics like jewelry, you might want to give prayerful study to what Paul says in 1 Corinthians 6:12-20 about the body being a temple of the Holy Spirit. Much has to do with sexual purity.

In writing to a man who had been committing adultery, Ellen White included this warning against breaking God's law:

Instead of bearing in your countenance a calm serenity under trial and affliction, like faithful Enoch, having your face radiant with hope and that peace which passeth understanding, you will stamp your countenance with carnal thoughts, with lustful desires (*Testimonies for the Church*, vol. 2, page 92).

One of the three qualities Paul emphasized in 1 Timothy 2:9,10 is modesty. Among Seventh-day Adventists ten different people probably would define that word, as applied to dress, ten different ways. My dictionary has two basic definitions: (1) not vain or boastful, unassuming, and (2) behaving, dressing, speaking, etc. in a way that is considered proper, decorous, decent.

At Andrews University, as spring comes quite a number of the girls begin to wear less and less, particularly with abbreviated shorts and immodest skirts. In early May one year I was seated at a cafeteria table with two fellows and three girls. One of the fellows, who had been at Oakwood, commented, "We are seeing a lot more flesh these days," and added, "At Oakwood shorts are not allowed."

One young man commented, "I think short shorts on women are blatant self-promotion." I said nothing, but thought, "It might be more accurate to say, "blatant sex-promotion." In treating the subject of modesty, we do well to remember, Whether shorts, low cut dresses, split skirts, or whatever, the carnal nature of most men seeks to see all that can be seen.

Along with Paul's focus on modesty, sensibility, and attractiveness, we could add this, with clothes as with food and other things, "Whether you eat or drink or whatever you do, do all to the glory of God" (1 Corinthians 10:31).

Against that principle, test an article in the South Bend *Tribune* for July 29, 1998, about soon-to-come casual men's wear. It began like this: "The clothes are just on the cutting edge of bad taste: widened-bottomed and turned up jeans, denim hot-pants, sequined shirts, sandals, tight T-shirts with mesh tank tops. The hats look like German beer-parlor wear" (page D1).

Resisting popular customs takes a lot of God's help, plus a conscience well aware of scriptural teachings. Then through prayer, the study of God's Word, and a sense of God's presence, obedience becomes a delight rather than a distasteful requirement.

Begin with yourself. Remind yourself that a temple is not only a sacred place; God intends that it also be beautiful—that it inspire awe and wonder.

TESTING, TESTING, TESTING

Along with vegetarianism, amusements, and music, the topic of clothes always has been controversial. The only solution is to go to Scripture, then to you knees in prayer, and asking, "What would Jesus choose for me? What is God's will?"

Here are possible study and discussion options:

- *Study Romans 12:1, 2 in several versions. Then add verse 3. What principles that apply to this chapter do you find?*
- *Compare the topics in this chapter with John 7:17; 8:12; 8:28, 29; 8:50; and Philippians 4:8 with Philippians 2:5-11. Then make a list of basic principles you find in these passages.*

Chapter 20

A Passion for Compassion

"When Jesus went out He saw a great multitude;
and He was moved with compassion for them,
and healed their sick."
(Matthew 14:14)

He was moved with compassion. "Filled with pity," the TEV words it. "Very deeply moved," according to Phillips.

The dictionary defines compassion as sorrow for the sufferings or trouble of another or others, accompanied by an urge to help.

This is a story about a wedding dress, and about compassion:

"It was a beautiful wedding on a crisp December day, a week before Christmas," Barbara, the owner of the dress wrote. "It was a season of hope and joy."

As with so many marriages, the hope and joy didn't last. "I watched helplessly as my beloved succumbed to the grip of escalating alcoholism and the deceit that abides with it," Barbara continued. "I felt myself crumbling under the constant rain of emotional abuse. My energies revived only when that abuse began to turn its ugly face toward our two tiny children. Joy and hope were gone; the marriage was in shambles. The wedding dress, carefully packed away in memory of a happier time, became a source of pain."

At the hospital where Barbara worked as a nurse, Teresa, twenty-seven, was dying of cancer. At her side was her beloved fiancé. The joy that she had dreamed about was ebbing away. He, too, was shattered by the grim reality that their life together would not be.

As morphine dripped through the intravenous line, Teresa whispered to Barbara, "My fiancé and I have decided to get married before I die. I know that may not make sense, but we want to be one before God, even if for only a short time. I don't know how we would get married here though."

"Let me talk to our chaplain," Barbara said.

The chapel at the hospital was reserved, the chaplain counseled with the couple about the meaning of marriage, and the social worker—a gifted violinist—offered to play for the ceremony. The hospital cafeteria would prepare a reception.

"I guess I'll look kind of strange in this hospital gown," Teresa said to Barbara. Her funds had been exhausted; her hospitalization was covered by state insurance for the indigent.

"I have a lovely dress you could wear," Barbara told Teresa. "I wore it for my wedding, and I think it would fit you."

As Barbara described the dress and the delicate matching veil, Teresa's eyes sparkled.

THE WEDDING DAY DAWNS

The wedding day dawned with clear sunshine; an undercurrent of joy pervaded the hospital floor. The wedding dress hung at the foot of Teresa's bed. Teresa waited contentedly, a soft smile framing her gaunt face.

A local florist had donated a bouquet of pink roses, and at 1:00 p.m. Barbara entered the room to begin dressing the bride. As she picked up the dress, her thoughts went back to her own wedding day. She touched the fabric, enjoying its smoothness. As she turned to Teresa, she noted how peaceful she looked.

"Teresa, are you ready to be a beautiful bride?" Barbara asked. Then, "Teresa? Teresa! Oh no. Please, God, not now. Don't let her die right now!"

Teresa glanced briefly at Barbara, and gently smiled goodbye.

Teresa's fiancé sobbed uncontrollably as he threw himself on her frail body. Her mother slumped at the end of the bed, while Barbara's tears splashed onto the wedding dress that she held.

Two days later Teresa's mother and her fiancé sought out Barbara to invite her to the funeral. "Teresa loved you," her mother said. "We would be honored if you could be with us at the funeral. She wanted so much to be a bride, and you understood."

She wanted so much to be a bride. Barbara thought.

"My Teresa would have been beautiful in that dress," her mother added.

If not beautiful in life, why not in death? Barbara mused. *Then, No, Lord, no. That's too much.*

A statement of Paul came to mind: "My purpose is that they may be encouraged in heart and united in love so that they may have the full riches of complete understanding" (Colossians 2:2, NIV).

"What to you mean, Lord?" Barbara asked.

"Encourage them in heart and show them My love through your love."

With faltering voice Barbara asked, "How will Teresa be dressed for the funeral?"

Teresa's mother averted her eyes, then said, "We haven't decided yet. All her clothes are so old and too big for her now."

"Would you like to dress Teresa in her wedding dress?" Barbara asked.

"But that is your wedding dress," her fiancé said.

"No, it was my wedding dress, but it was also to be Teresa's wedding dress. It's her dress. You may have it."

In concluding her story Barbara Frye wrote:

"Teresa was buried in the creamy white satin dress with tiny pearls. A filmy matching veil gently covered her face, still delicate in death. I stood at her gravesite, trying to understand the mystery of God's ways. 'Oh, the depth of the riches of the wisdom and knowledge of God! How unsearchable his judgments, and his paths beyond tracing out' (Rom. 11:33, 34, NIV)"— Condensed and adapted from the June 1996 NAD edition of the *Adventist Review*.

Jesus was moved with compassion. Blessed are all who are likewise moved!

A PASSION FOR COMPASSION

One Sabbath afternoon, after a time of prayer in the outdoors, I stopped at Chan Shun Hall on the Andrews campus to get a drink. I heard music in the auditorium, looked in, and decided to stay. It was a group of graduating dietetics students, and after the music a speaker stood. Nutritionist Evelyn Cole Kissenger launched into a message titled "Preparation, Passion, and Prayer."

Evelyn is a stay-at-home mom who home schools her four children. She also works part time teaching nutrition. With her permission, I'd like to share a little of what she brought out as she discussed preparation, then a passion to help, and then prayer.

Prepare. "Success," Evelyn said, "is when preparation meets opportunity." She cited, "Your ears shall hear a voice behind you saying, 'This is the way; walk in it' " (Isaiah 30:21).

From her own experience, she told how as a single parent she had moved to Andrews. By taking a class or two each quarter she earned a masters in business, which she hoped to use for wellness programs in Berrien Country. She taught classes in nutrition for pregnant mothers, and encouraged breast-feeding. She had prepared, and doors of opportunity were beginning to open.

"This spring," she said, "I was involved in a wellness program at Borgess Hospital in Kalamazoo. There were 500 participants. It is so exciting to see how lifestyle choices can make a difference in people's lives in just three to four weeks."

Be passionate. She urged this for three areas:

- Be passionate about your profession. The possibilities are limitless. Get involved. Network. Whatever you do, do your best.
- Be passionate about your personal health. As a nutritionist, practice what you preach. The greatest gift you can give yourself, your family, your profession, your community, and your country is a healthy you.
- Be passionate about being compassionate. People don't care about how much you know, until they know how much you care. The way you treat others matters.

How do you develop compassion? Watch Jesus. Read the Gospels, *The Desire of Ages*, *The Ministry of Healing*. Ask, What makes Jesus the way He is? How can I be more like Him?

Fill your life with prayer. When you pray, you have a powerful Partner. I have seen people change before my eyes. A woman will drag her husband to nutrition counseling because of elevated lab values, high cholesterol, high triglycerides, overweight. He obviously doesn't want to be there.

I begin praying double time for God to soften his heart and to help him be receptive. As the session continues, I notice a softening and a greater interest in the idea of taking better care of himself. As he leaves he seems genuinely appreciative of our time together.

While working in the hospital, I often would enter a room and talk to a patient about what they eat. When we talk about nutrition, many other life issues seem to ooze out. So many times the burdens are so great, I send up prayers for wisdom as to what to say. Leaving the room, I think back and realize God gave me the words I spoke.

THINKING ABOUT COMPASSION

- *If you are studying this chapter in a small group, you might share with each other the most striking example of compassion that has come to your notice.*
- *What Bible examples of the compassion of Jesus do you recall?*
- *In words about Jesus, the first page of the first chapter of* The Ministry of Healing *says, "His compassion knew no limit" (page 17). If you have access to the book, you will be thrilled by the first chapter.*
- *What ideas from this chapter might you use with members of your own family, or with co-workers?*

Chapter 21

A Passion for Lost People

"You were not redeemed with corruptible things,
like silver and gold . . . but with the precious blood of Christ."
(1 Peter 1:18, 19)

When Jataija Wall was born on October 8, 1997, three months premature, she weighed 12.5 ounces. That appears to make her the smallest baby ever to survive without major brain, lung, or other organ damage.

"We thought readers would like to know how she is doing," the June 22, 1998 issue of *U.S. News and World Report* said in an article titled, "The tiniest known preemie is doing fine."

The Wall family lives in Cleveland, Ohio. At seven months Jataija was only 7 pounds, 2 ounces, but developmentally, she appeared to be right on schedule, *U.S. News and World Report* reported. "She's very alert, very sociable. She's pretty much where we expect her to be," said Marc Collin, Medical director of the neonatal intensive care unit at MetroHealth.

About two hundred thousand dollars in hospital charges went into saving her.

Nobody would begrudge a penny of that. A human life is precious. And a person won to Christ becomes even more precious.

Consider the above statement from 1 Peter. In human experience the value of an object generally equals the price paid for it. That fact of life makes your eternal worth equal to the value of the blood of Christ. The author of *The Desire of Ages*, in a comment about Jesus weeping over Jerusalem, says, "One soul is of such value that, in comparison with it, worlds sink into insignificance" (page 578).

Against the background of what Peter wrote, we can declare that one person saved for Christ is worth more than ten thousand worlds. In this chapter and the next I want to introduce you to young people who believe that.

MEET GONI

One is Antigoni Varahidis, a sophomore nursing student at Andrews University. At fourteen she was an atheist. Now at twenty she has a passion to testify about two things:

- What Christ has done for her
- Her burden to share the gospel with every person she possibly can reach

God has been opening doors for her to do that. One evening in April 1998, Goni's roommate, Tricia, asked her, "What have you done for God recently?" For a time they discussed their desire to testify for Christ. Then after they both had gone to bed, Goni lay there thinking.

"It's a miracle—a lot of miracles—that I'm here. I'd love to share my testimony at one of our weekly chapel services at the church. But chapel speakers for this quarter have already been selected, so there's no chance."

The next morning she got a phone call. It was Kari Gibbs, a student leader from the Honors Department. "On May 5, Honors has chapel," Kari told Goni. "Would you be the speaker?"

Goni accepted, then slipped to her knees. "Dear Father," she prayed, "I don't want to be seen. I want Your name to be honored. Help me to say what You want me to say."

What follows are some questions I asked Goni after reviewing a video of her chapel talk.

INTERVIEWING GONI

1. Goni, did you grow up with any kind of religious faith?

Yes. My parents are Greek Orthodox, though they don't attend church often. When I was a child Mom sometimes dragged me to church, but I hated it. I hated school, too, and one time I beat up a classmate, and the principal called the police.

2. What was your childhood like?

I was a tough girl, with no thought of God. One day I was talking with a guy at his car. He told me, "Goni, I have come to the conclusion that there is no God." I told him, "That's what I believe, too." From then on I gave no thought to religion.

I went into the club scene, and would stay out all night and then sleep till mid-afternoon. During my teens the only person I felt close to was John, a brother six years older than I.

Then one morning, I heard my dad screaming, "Our baby is dead! Our baby is dead!" He had gone into the garage, and the car was running. My brother was slumped over on the seat. He had committed suicide.

3. What happened next in your life?

I became cold as ice. My heart turned to stone. I cared for no one.

4. How did you learn about Seventh-day Adventists?

I began working at my uncle's donut shop. One of my cousins also worked there, and she and her husband had been studying a Daniel seminar. They invited me to join them. I found it fascinating.

I started reading the New Testament. As I read it, I met a Man—a Man like no one I had ever known. He was whipped, He was crucified—for me. That melted my hard heart. I stopped clubbing, stopped staying out all night, and began to study for baptism.

5. What gives you the burden you now have to reach other young people?

I had an experience spring break (1998) that really influenced me. I had gone home to Toronto. There was a fellow I had met at church who was turned off on spiritual things. The Lord impressed me, "Goni, you should call him and try to encourage him." That happened several times, but I kept putting it off.

Three weeks later, he was murdered. He had been in downtown Toronto and met some fellows who took a dislike to him. He started to run, and they chased him. They caught up with him on a busy street corner, at a bus stop. They stabbed him in the back, right in front of dozens of people. He died a few days later.

I will never forget how the Lord had repeatedly impressed me to call him right up to the day before.

6. What does Bible study mean to you, Goni?

It's interesting that you ask. When I was first converted I'd spend at least an hour a day. I slacked off, but right now I'm in the Maga-book program here in Toronto, and God is bringing me back to my first love.

7. What do you see as your greatest goal right now, Goni?

To see my Savior and bring as many people as possible to heaven with me. I want to see everyone on fire for God. There's enough of us—the youth—that if God really controlled us He could use us to bring everything to a finish.

CHRIST WANTS ALL

In Luke 15 Christ told three parables to make two points:

- Every person matters to God
- He doesn't want to lose a single person

A shepherd had ninety-nine of his one hundred sheep, and went out into the night to find the missing one. A woman had nine of her ten coins but diligently hunted for the missing one. A father prayed almost continually for a wandering son to come home.

Years ago, as I was going through the Ellen White devotional book titled *That I May Know Him,* I came across a two sentence statement that has haunted me ever since. It was a comment on Isaiah 53:4, 5—the passage about Christ being wounded for our sins. It said this: "Christ wanted all. He could not endure that one should be lost" (page 67).

The entire fifty-third chapter of Isaiah tells what Christ was willing to suffer. And He would have done it for me alone, for you alone! *He still wants all— He cannot endure the thought that even one should be lost!*

Give me, O God, a passion like that!

Do you want that kind of passion too? If you are new to the church you most likely still have your first love. Would you join me in a commitment to do three things?

1. Remember that prayer is the first step toward winning family members, friends, neighbors, and co-workers to Christ.

Keep reviewing the seven certainties about prayer summarized in chapter 14. Be encouraged, also, from this truth brought out in chapter 15: God accepts every desire for the salvation of another as a prayer. In Romans 10:1 Paul said, "Brethren, my heart's desire and prayer to God for Israel is that they may be saved." Even Paul's desire God thought of as a prayer.

As previously noted, "When engaged in our daily labor, we may breathe out our heart's desire, inaudible to any human ear; but that word cannot die away into silence, nor can it be lost. Nothing can drown the soul's desire. . . . It is God to whom we are speaking, and our prayer is heard" (*Messages to Young People,* page 250).

Every such desire, every such prayer, has an influence for good, and God records it in His book of remembrance (Malachi 3:16).

2. Keep strengthening your faith with much time in God's Word.

Spend time with some of the prayers of the Bible. Over a period of time, one by one, commit some to memory. Then use them in your coming and going. I have been richly blessed by memorizing and using the following prayers of Paul: Ephesians 3:14-19, Philippians 1:9-11, and Colossians 1:9-14.

Many of the psalms are prayers. I especially recommend Psalm 67 as a good one to memorize and pray in behalf of getting the gospel to all the world. Psalm 72:18, 19 and Psalm 90:16, 17 make excellent petitions for youth to use when praying for fellow youth.

3. Be alert to minister to the needs of others, and through ministry win their confidence.

Use Christ's methods. Whenever He could, He talked to individuals, as with Nicodemus and the woman at the well. Study this summary statement about His method: "The Saviour mingled with men as one who desired their good. He showed His sympathy for them, ministered to their needs, and won their confidence. Then He bade them, 'Follow Me' " (*The Ministry of Healing,* page 143).

USABLE IDEAS

- *Spend some devotional time with the three parables about seeking the lost as told in Luke 15. As you meditate and pray, ask God to give you an ever increasing passion for lost people.*

- *In every religion class I teach at Andrews, I ask students to memorize Psalm 90:16, 17 as a prayer to use when praying for other youth. By writing it on a 3-by-5 card and keeping it with you, you can do something similar.*

- *I also ask students to memorize Ephesians 3:14-19 and then use it in praying for others. I do the same with Philippians 1:9-11. You might want to start with one of these rather than Psalm 90:16, 17.*

- *Prayerfully study the above summary of Christ's methods for winning people. Let it guide you as you seek to win others to Him.*

Chapter 22

Christ's Passion: To Share His Joy

"Enter into the joy of your lord. . . . Enter into the joy of your lord."
(Matthew 25:21, 23)

The above invitation of Christ, from His talents parable, raises two questions:

- What is "the joy of your lord"?
- How does one enter into that joy?

The three parables of Jesus in Luke 15—the lost sheep, the lost coin, and the lost son—all end with rejoicing from finding the lost. "Likewise, I say to you, there is joy in the presence of the angels of God over one sinner who repents" (Luke 15:10). The joy of the Lord is the thrill that surges through His heart when the lost is found.

How do we enter into that joy? By becoming "laborers together with God" (1 Corinthians 3:9). When you help a family member or friend find Christ, the joy of the Lord thrills you; in eternity it will excite you even more.

On this August 2, 1998—my last day to get the final three chapters of this manuscript finished, I awoke early and took a two-mile prayer walk. As I prayed, I reminded myself that in the Seventh-day Adventist Church we have 81 colleges and universities, 930 secondary schools, and 4,500 elementary schools—for a total of 900,000 youth. I think of all of them in the light of this paragraph from *Education* about what Adventist education ought to be producing:

> With such an army of workers as our youth, rightly trained, might furnish, how soon the message of a crucified, risen, and soon-coming Saviour might be carried to the whole world! How soon might the end come—the end of suffering, sorrow, and sin! (page 271).

Rightly trained. Whatever else right training should include, three things are imperatives, namely, an education that helps students become eager to study the Bible, one that helps them experience meaningful prayer, and one that helps them discover ministries for which they have a talent and which they enjoy.

A MINISTRY EXAMPLE

Near the beginning of the 1996–97 school year, two Andrews students, William Hurtado and Heidi Towar, prayed that God would help them get ministries started in Benton Harbor, a city of 15,000 some twelve miles from Andrews that consists largely of low-income and welfare recipient citizens.

The January 28, 1997, South Bend *Tribune* reported that in an eleven-day span in late December and early January, ten people had been murdered in Benton Harbor, and that Attorney General Janet Reno would be sending an FBI team into the area to help deal with the crime wave taking place there.

In spite of possible hazards, a ministry group that has grown from just a few to scores of students now drives to Benton Harbor every Sabbath afternoon to do street ministry and a health ministry, give Bible studies, conduct two story hours for children, and visit with patients in a nursing home.

About twenty or twenty-five students meet in the student center on Friday afternoons from 5:30 to 6:30 to pray for Benton Harbor and to share experiences from the previous Sabbath afternoon. Then from 6:30 to 7:00 they meet in their various ministry groups to plan for the next day. Whenever possible I have attended the testimony and prayer part of this meeting. I have been awed again and again by the reflection of Christ that I see in the faces of this circle of young adults.

Here are some questions I asked:

1. How did the Benton Harbor ministries get started?

One Sabbath during the fall of 1996, Pastor Dwight preached a sermon in which he said, "We need to come to the place where what breaks the heart of God breaks our heart also." That afternoon six of us drove to Benton Harbor to look for opportunities to minister. We did some door to door visitation just to get acquainted.

The next Sabbath there were twelve. Eventually God opened the door so that we could get the Benton Harbor Street Ministry Center building. It has kept growing until we now sometimes have a hundred people out doing various kinds of ministries.

2. What kinds of ministries do students do on a typical Sabbath?

We have a story hour, which usually attracts fifty or more youngsters. Then there is the street ministry, going door to door meeting people, asking if they have prayer requests, or if they would like to study the Bible. We go to a nursing home to visit and pray with people there. We have a health ministry, where a van parks in a shopping center and takes blood pressures. We give Bible studies, and have a church-planting goal.

3. What kind of activities do students do at the two story hours to hold attention?

Singing, stories, crafts, games, things like at Vacation Bible schools. Our students also establish bonds with the children. It's not unusual to see a child hugging the girl he or she has established a bond with.

4. Benton Harbor has a major crime problem. Does that make Andrews students nervous?

Surprisingly, for middle-class students, there is no fear at all. We do urge caution: never go alone, keep mixed gender, tell where you are going, use common sense, avoid alcohol-infested areas.

On Friday evenings many of our participants meet in the student center to study the Bible, pray, and plan the next-day activities. There are also other planning sessions, which always include much prayer.

5. What effects has the involvement had on the academy and college youth who go?

I have seen several students change from lethargic, not attending church, not comfortable talking about God, now not only helping but wanting to lead.

YOUTH IN PUBLIC SCHOOL

Becoming rightly trained applies with equal force to children and youth in public school. That task rests upon parents and upon Sabbath School teachers and other adults. To bring about the training God desires will require moving forward on our knees and helping our children and youth who attend public school to experience enjoyable prayer, Bible study, and ministry.

In order to interest children in the Bible, as parents we must show interest in it ourselves. The same goes for prayer, both private and as a family. Abraham modeled this; wherever he went he set up a family altar. For most families morning worship needs to be brief; evening worship generally can be a little longer.

The book *Messages to Young People* sums up what evening worships should be like: "At an early hour of the evening, when we can pray unhurriedly and understandingly, we should present our supplications and raise our voices in happy, grateful praise" (page 342).

To keep worships from being dry, tedious, or irksome, the one leading out needs to put thought into the preparation. With variety, worships can be intensely interesting to the children and, to all, the most pleasant and enjoyable time of the day.

Variety is crucial. When I was putting together a 166-page *Faith and Prayer Syllabus*, I taught a seminary class that we called The Ministry of Prayer. One day in class I asked students to share what they did in their families to make worships interesting. Along with the usual, here are four of the twelve suggestions from the students, in greatly condensed form, of course:

1. In families with small children, use several Sabbath afternoons to prepare a worship notebook. For each page include a theme, a song, a text, a picture, a story or poem, and for small children a finger play or other participatory items. Then from time to time, at worship, let children take turns choosing the page for the evening.

2. Occasionally prepare a worship built around music, using varied family talents. Unless a Friday evening, use only two or three songs, along with a couple of verses from a praise psalm, and prayer.

3. Develop a slide or video presentation to use occasionally. Build it around a cherished memory—a vacation trip, a birthday, etc. Numerous

nature videos are available; generally use only a small section unless it is for a Friday or Sabbath evening.

4. Occasionally conduct a thanksgiving service, with each person telling one thing that happened that day that he or she is thankful for.

Under the section titled "Personal and Family Prayer," the syllabus has sixteen one- or two-page topics, such as "Scheduling Time to Pray," "How to Keep Secret Prayer Refreshing," "Praying as We Go About Our Work," "Teaching Children Good Devotional Habits," etc. It can be secured from HART Research Center, Fallbrook, California, or ordered from HART through your Adventist Book Center.

A second need will be to get well acquainted with books like Education *and* Counsels to Parents, Teachers, and Students—*and then as far as possible applying principles taught there in our homes and churches.*

The 320-page book *Education* has nine sections, beginning with "First Principles," "Illustrations," "The Master Teacher," and "Nature Teaching." The section "Nature Teaching" alone is worth the price of the book.

The book *Counsels to Parents, Teachers, and Students* is first of all for parents. The twenty-four sections in its 575 pages are a gold mine! As a resource for parents nothing equals it.

ENTERING INTO CHRIST'S JOY

Let's project time ahead to when the wonder-filled future described in Revelation 21 and 22 becomes reality:

O what a scene of rejoicing it will be when the Lamb of God shall place upon the heads of the redeemed the victor's crown! Never, never more will you be led into temptation and sin. You will see the King in His beauty. And those you have helped heavenward will meet you there. They will throw their arms about you and acknowledge what you have done for them. "You watched over me," they will say; "you prayed for me; you helped me to gain heaven" (*In Heavenly Places*, page 280).

As you seek to apply ideas, you have a lot to choose from. A few options include:

*   *Whether a student, a parent, a Sabbath School teacher, an educator, or whoever, in your imagination put yourself into the preceding paragraph.*

Spend a few moments thinking about how you will feel at that time.

- *This chapter suggests that the end product in the right kind of education are students who (1) are eager to study the Bible, (2) are experiencing meaningful prayer, and (3) have discovered ministries that they enjoy. Discuss in a small group how the ministry part could be made more effective in your local church.*

- *The book* Education *has a chapter titled "Faith and Prayer." Take some of your devotional time to read that chapter, and possibly discuss it with a family member or friend.*

Education has eight chapters in the section "The Bible as an Educator." Try to read a chapter at a time, and as you read underline what you see as usable ideas.

Chapter 23

The Choice of the Trees

"He who is not with Me is against Me,
and he who does not gather with Me scatters abroad."
(Matthew 12:30)

Jesus came starkly to the point: anyone not *with* Him is against Him. There is no middle ground in the great controversy. We are with Christ—*with* suggests wholeheartedly—or we are against Him. Not to choose is to choose.

The first weekend of March 1998, Delinda Snyder, a sophomore at Andrews University, borrowed her brother's car and left campus with a Bible, a notebook, and a large jug of water. Taking no food, she went into the woods for two days to fast, to pray, and to prepare a talk about a decision for or against Christ. Her message, drawn from the two thieves crucified with Jesus, was to have been given on the last chapel of the winter quarter of the 1997–98 school year.

The entire series had been about choices, and Delinda's presentation had been scheduled for Tuesday, March 10. But on Monday, March 9, after nearly six weeks with no snow, a blizzard roared in. On Tuesday, roads were impassable, and all schools and businesses in Southwest Michigan were shut down.

Early in this book we focused on full surrender to Christ, as summarized here: "Surrender means the uttermost giving up of all we have and are to the mastery of Jesus—our worst, our best, our possessions, our past, our future, our life plans, our loved ones, our will, our *self.* That is surrender" (A. G. Daniells, *A Leader of Men,* page 91).

Such a surrender opens the door for everything God offers in this pledge: "I promise that I will bless you with everything I have—bless and bless and bless!" (Hebrews 6:14, The Message). If you are hesitating about that kind of surrender, perhaps this message that Delinda had no opportunity to share with her peers because of the blizzard can still speak. What follows is a condensed version taken from the copy she had on her computer:

Let's go to Genesis 2: "Then the Lord God took the man and put him in the garden of Eden to dress and keep it, And the Lord commanded the man, saying, 'Of every tree in the garden you may freely eat; but of the tree of the knowledge of good and evil you shall not eat, for in the day that you eat of it you shall surely die' " (verses 15-17).

Adam and Eve's freedom was based upon a tree. There in the middle of the garden stood their choice. All other choices boiled down to one choice. Just one choice. The choice of a tree. The tree of knowledge of good and evil. To eat the forbidden fruit was a choice for death. To obey the words of God would result in eternal happiness. The choice belonged to them.

Eve chose to eat the forbidden fruit. Then Adam chose to also eat the fruit. He chose to go against what God had told him as truth. Adam and Eve chose to sin. And of course there was a consequence. "You will die," God had said.

There in a garden the choice was made. That's it. End of the story. The human race is condemned to die because of the choice Adam and Eve made.

But wait a minute. That's not it. There is another choice. There is another story; there is another garden, the Garden of Gethsemane. In that garden Jesus chose to hang on another tree. He would give us a second chance.

In the time of Christ the instrument for crucifixion was called a tree—a cursed tree. Taylor Bunch in *Behold the Man* said this about the cross:

It is said that the use of the cross as an instrument of punishment had its origin in the ancient practice of fastening a criminal "to a tree, which was termed accursed, but was later known as 'the cross.' " The cross was therefore still spoken of as a "tree" in the days of the apostles (page 167).

The word *cross* referred to what it looked like, and *tree* referred to what it really was. Regardless of what you call it, the fact remains that it was made from a once strong, healthy tree. A good tree had to be cut down; it had to change from a green, living tree to a brown, dead beam. Its source of life was cut off.

And that was the whole point of crucifixion—to take a living human being and cut off their source of life. Crucifixion turned a tree, if you will, a person, into a brown lifeless body.

WHAT DOES THIS MEAN FOR US?

That's past; what does it mean to us today? Let's turn to Luke 23:39, "Then one of the criminals who were hanged blasphemed Him, saying, 'If you are the Christ save Yourself and us.' "

What's a criminal? Someone who breaks the rules, the law. Both these guys were robbers. They had stolen, they had broken the law, they didn't measure up to the standard.

So what's the standard we must measure up to? To follow God's commands. Have we? No. We've failed. Look at Romans 3:23, "For all have sinned and fall short of the glory of God." So we are all criminals; we've broken the rules.

Now look again at the last part of Luke 23:39, at the insults, "If You are the Christ, save Yourself and us." Why did this criminal join in the mockery? They were in this crucifixion thing together. You would think there would be a sense of camaraderie. Why did he turn on the very person who understood what he was going through? Why?

Let me ask you another question. Where was this criminal's focus? On himself. "I'm in pain. I don't want to be in pain. I don't want to die. That's all I care about, myself."

Have you ever prayed that kind of prayer? I have. There was this conflict I had with another person. I was going to their house to work it out. But I didn't want to. I prayed they would not be home. My prayer was completely selfish. I just wanted out of a difficult situation.

So with the first criminal. He was concerned only for himself. He didn't care about anyone or anything else.

Now look at the second criminal. He rebuked the first criminal. He stood up for Jesus. He could have just said, "Jesus, I believe You are the Son of God." But He defended Jesus. He looked at Jesus, all contorted, blood engulfing every part of His body, half naked, but He saw a King. He took the focus off himself and focused on Jesus.

Are we willing to do that? Are we willing to stand up for Jesus when everyone else is making fun of Him?

TWO OPTIONS

Two criminals. One choice. Each made his decision. One chose Christ. One did not. We too are criminals. We too have a choice. It's the choice of the trees. Which tree are we going to choose? The tree in Eden, the tree of disobedience? Or the tree upon which Jesus hangs?

One choice. Two options. What are you going to choose? Are you going to focus on yourself or are you going to focus on Christ?

What does all this choosing mean, though? Look again at verses 42 and 43. "Lord, remember me when you come into Your kingdom." And Christ's response: "You will be with Me in paradise."

What's paradise? I looked it up in the commentary. It said a paradise is a forest, an orchard, or a preserve containing trees. Then I looked it up in the original Greek. It said paradise means a garden. So rephrasing what Christ said, "I tell you the truth today, you will be with Me in the garden." Jesus promised this guy the Garden of God.

Christ also promises us the Garden of God if we choose Him. Adam and Eve blew it. They made the wrong choice in the Garden of Eden. We are living in sin as a result of their choice. But we have a choice to make too. God wants to bring us back to the garden. Not back to the garden with the tree of the knowledge of good and evil, but to the Garden of God.

The battle for this world started at a tree. It started at the tree of knowledge of good and evil. And the battle for this world ended at a tree—the cross Jesus hung upon. But God doesn't want to stop there. He wants to bring us home. He wants to take us to the Tree of Life.

Revelation 2:7 tells us what will happen if we choose Christ. "To Him who overcomes [to him who chooses] I will give to eat from the tree of life, which is in the midst of the Paradise of God." Not to a garden with a tree of knowledge of good and evil, but to the Garden of God with the tree of life.

Then the choices will have been made. The decision process will be over. In the book *Education*, Ellen White says this: "Not all the conditions in that first school of Eden will be found in the future life. No tree of knowledge of good and evil will afford opportunity for temptation. No tempter is there, no possibility of wrong. Every character has withstood the testing of evil, and none are any longer susceptible to its power" (page 302).

WHICH CRIMINAL?

But that's the future. That's after the decisions have been made. Adam and Eve made their choice at the tree of good and evil(that's past. What's the here and now? We must choose which criminal we are going to be. Are we going to focus upon ourselves like the first criminal did, or are we going to focus on Jesus like the second criminal did?

Yourself or Christ? The choice must be made, for God is a God who honors the freedom of choice. He's not going to take that away from you.

Delinda concluded her talk by giving her own testimony:

"This past weekend I answered that question. After going 42 hours without eating, feeling so faint I could hardly stand up, it hit me. Jesus Christ went through far more than this for me. Even though His body was screaming out in pain and fatigue He still chose to go ahead with His plan. He chose the cursed tree so that I might have the tree of life.

"This past weekend I chose to take the focus off myself and place it on Him. Yeah, I really wanted to focus on my stomach that was craving food. But I stopped focusing on my own wants and desires and focused on Him.

"The time is now. The choice is before us."

MAKING APPLICATION

God loved. God gave (John 3:16). Jesus gave. "He gave all there was of Himself" (*In Heavenly Places*, page 43).

"Choose for yourselves this day whom you will serve" (Joshua 24:15). "Look away from self to Jesus. Embrace Him as your Saviour" (*In Heavenly Places*, page 116).

As you think and pray, here are some suggestions:

- *Review again the definition of surrender given at the start of this chapter. If you have not already made it, what would it take for you to do so? As you think and pray, see what Paul says in 2 Corinthians 6:1, 2.*

- *Something to pray about: "Trustful dependence on Jesus makes victory not only possible but certain" (*In Heavenly Places, *page 17).*
- *The Bible contains numerous appeals. Check out a few: Deuteronomy 30:19, 20; Isaiah 55:6, 7; Matthew 11:28-30; Revelation 22:17.*
- *More to pray about: "Talk faith, live faith, cultivate love to God. . . . Magnify His holy name. Tell of His goodness; talk of His mercy, and tell of His power" (*Our High Calling, *page 20).*

Chapter 24

Leaders for a New Century

"Let no one despise your youth,
but be an example to the believers in word,
in conduct, in love, in spirit, in faith, in purity."
(1 Timothy 4:12)

"On March 3, 1988, we (Jennifer and Shasta) were bumping along in Shasta's clunker car, talking about wedding plans and how busy we were with everything in our lives. Somehow the talk turned to the reputation of our generation."

That's how a fax from Shasta Emery Burr of La Sierra University began. She went on to say:

"We are both tired of listening to the church try to figure out 'creative' ways to keep us from leaving the church. We both agreed that nothing can save us from leaving, except ourselves. Only we can decide that. We laughed about how cool it would be if our entire generation (which has been labeled X) would come together to make a commitment for ourselves to God by dedicating our generation to His service. The SDA church needs us in a lot of ways—and we need to start stepping up and helping in whatever small ways we can."

Before citing more from Shasta's fax, an explanation: I was trying to find out about something called eXcite98. I first heard about this exciting development from Dr. Ed Karlow, physics teacher at La Sierra University. I met him in the cafeteria at Andrews University near the end of July 1998, but I had known him before when he was a sixth-grader at Glendale Academy back in the 1950s. As we ate, I asked about the spiritual tone at La Sierra University. "It's absolutely incredible what has happened!" he exclaimed. "I have never seen anything like it. We have had some student leaders whom God has used to radically change the spiritual climate. A year ago, for example, we had only a half dozen student missionaries going out. This next year we will have forty."

He then told me about Shasta Emery (now Burr) and Jennifer Tyner—two young adults who had been working to organize an event called eXcite98. I called Shasta to find out more, and she faxed information about it. Here's more from her fax:

"So we went home laughing at how awesome that might be someday. But neither of us slept that night. And the next morning we both felt stupid for how excited we had each become overnight for something that 'couldn't happen.' "

THINGS BEGAN TO HAPPEN

"Hesitantly," Shasta continued, "we admitted to each other that we believed it actually needed to happen. And it needed to happen soon. God had touched us both with immense energy and hope that He would make it happen.

"We called everyone we knew to bounce it off them. And before we knew it, the decision wasn't whether or not it would happen—it was a matter of who, when, what, why, and where! We put our lives on hold and stayed up late every night to turn all the brainstorms into reality! Now brainstorms are coming from every direction, and we just sit in amazement every day as God brings new people, ideas, and energy into the movement."

The when and where were soon settled; it would be August 6-9, 1998, at La Sierra University, Riverside, California.

"We meet every day for prayer," Shasta continued. "And everyday, we hear of more and more wonderful stories from people who have left the church, but feel a need to come. Or from people who work for the church but want to be fulfilled. Or young couples who only go to church because of their kids, but now they want to take care of their own spirituality."

She then concluded, "People from our generation are coming together—all types. And together, we will grow in our own spiritual relationships, but as a whole, we will dedicate our generation to God and the mission of the SDA church."

More about what actually did happen in chapter 25. But, first, a few words about what I see as top priorities for all leaders as we enter the first decade of the next century:

GIVE PRAYER TOP PRIORITY.

The August 1998 issue of the North American edition of the *Adventist Review* was titled "Time to Seek the Lord." In an introductory editorial William Johnsson suggested:

> Among the various aspects that belong in seeking the Lord—repentance, confession, fasting, setting matters right, a love for the unsaved— one stands out as preeminent: prayer. Every other element depends on personal, honest communion with God (page 3).

And not just private prayer, though that comes first. We also need to do as Jesus suggested in Matthew 18:18-20. Jesus said, "When one or two of you get together on anything at all and make a prayer of it, my Father in heaven goes into action. And when two or three get together because of me, you can be sure that I'll be there" (Matthew 18:19, 20, The Message).

God has long wanted to go into action by sending the latter rain. The priorities of Joel 2:12-17 need top attention: heart-searching, repentance, gathering together to pray. Then God can fulfill all the promises of the last half of Joel 2: gracious promises related to the giving of the latter rain. And the prominence of youth in Joel 2:28-30 indicates they will also help lead in repentance and prayer.

The blessings that come have been described by Charles Finney, as cited by Wesley Duewel in his *Mighty Prevailing Prayer:* "Nothing tends more to cement the hearts of Christians than praying together. Never do they love one another so well as when they witness the outpouring of each other's hearts in prayer" (page 131).

OTHER PRIORITIES

Other priorities, all of which I have brought into focus in this book, include:

- Seeking a sense of brokenness at the foot of the cross, looking up to the Saviour for salvation.
- Seeking a growing hatred for sin.
- Development of an implicit trust in Jesus for righteousness.
- A passion for oneness with our Father.
- A passion for purity in Christ.
- A passion for lost people.
- An ever-growing longing to think as Jesus thinks, to love what He loves, and to hate what He hates—to be like Him in every way.
- A cautious watchfulness against compromise and being drawn into the snares of gradualism.
- A growing longing for godliness that is found in being totally possessed by Jesus Christ.

A GENERAL CONFERENCE LEADER DREAMS

Elder Johnsson is not the only leader with dreams for our church. Back at the North American Division year-end meetings in 1994, Alfred McClure, the division president, gave a key-note message he titled "Leaders for a New Century." In it he shared this dream, as reported in the January 1995 NAD edition of the *Adventist Review: "My dream is that our era will be remembered as the time when God raised up a generation of godly leaders."* (Italics his.)

Elder McClure told of a fascinating study he had done about when the people of God had godly leaders—and when they didn't. He started with Rehoboam, of whom it was written: "He forsook the law of the Lord, and all Israel along with him" (2 Chronicles 12:1).

And so it went all through the history of Israel, and of Judah. Before being carried into captivity by the Assyrians in 722 B.C. Israel (the ten tribes in the north) had had twenty kings, all of whom were evil. Judah, until Jerusalem was destroyed by Nebuchadnezzar in 586 B.C., also had twenty rulers, twelve of whom were ungodly.

The few exceptions who sought the Lord, such as Jehoshaphat, had a remarkable influence for good. Of him Scripture records, "He went out again among the people from Beersheba to the mountains of Ephraim, and brought them back to the Lord God of their fathers" (2 Chronicles 19:4).

Elder McClure warned of what probably is the greatest danger facing the church today, that of compromise:

> Now, I want nothing I say tonight to imply a lack of confidence in the leaders of this division. But I know how strong are the forces of compromise. I know how swift are the whirlpools of conformity. I know how the devil singles *you* out for his special attacks, because he can take so many down if he takes you. I know how easy it is to take as our models that which is going on around us (*Adventist Review*, January 1996).

THE LITTLE BY LITTLE DANGER

Satan has fine-tuned what has become one of his most effective techniques to weaken both individuals and denominations: *gradualism*. He used it in the matter of Israel wanting a king: "that we also may be like all the nations" (1 Samuel 8:20). He used it to erode the power of the early church. A little at a time he got leaders and members to lessen differences between themselves and pagans. "Almost imperceptibly the customs of heathenism found their way into the Christian church" (*The Great Controversy*, page 49).

Could that be happening again? The current emphasis on building a relationship with Christ has blessed many, and always should be a top priority. But a relationship must include obedience, as Jesus Himself said, "If you love Me, keep My commandments" (John 14:15). "Man shall not live by bread alone, but by every word that proceeds from the mouth of God" (Matthew 4:4).

"Every word" includes lifestyle. Hasn't there been a tendency to say little or nothing about what we call standards, things that have to do with modesty, music, jewelry, competition in sports, Sabbath observance, and diet? Space permits only one example: the increased use of jewelry among us.

ADVICE FROM A METHODIST

Back in 1855, for example, the Methodist church manual, *Methodist Discipline*, asked, "Should we insist on rules concerning dress?" The reply? "By all means."

The context stated, "Receive none into the church until they have left off all superfluous ornaments. . . . Give no admission to those who wear rings" (page 88). But by 1872, according to Methodism's *The Doctrines of Discipline*, a wedding ring could be used "if the parties desire it." It remained that way until the 1930s, when the use of a ring in marriage ceremonies became standard for most Methodists.

Is it wise for us to follow in the steps of the Methodists and others who previously shunned jewelry?

In *Christian Dress and Adornment* Samuele Bacchiocchi cites advice from a Methodist named Dean M. Kelly, who had an article in *Adventists Affirm* titled "How Adventism Can Stop Growing." His advice? "Become like the Methodists" (Spring, 1991, page 56). According to Kelly, all that Adventists need to do to stop growing and start declining is to decide that church standards of dress, diet, jewelry, tithing, etc., are not really essential.

In summary, as new leaders come onto the stage of action, let's grow together in being totally like Jesus *in everything*.

IN APPLICATION

More and more like Jesus! Those of you new to Seventh-day Adventist beliefs still have your first love. Evaluate this chapter in the context of that love. For all, as you seek applications from the content of this chapter, here are a few options:

- *Give careful study to Joel 2:12-17, then compare it with the latter rain promises in verses 18-33. Why, in your opinion, must the events of verses 12-17 take place before the promises of verses 18-33?*
- *"Seek the Lord, all you meek of the earth, who have upheld His justice. Seek righteousness, seek humility" (Zeph. 2:3). Compare that with Joel 2:12-17. What significance do you see in the fact that Joel 2:28-30 gives a prominence to youth?*
- *Read again the introduction of this book, and then compare it with the following statement. Ask, "Do I feel this way?"*

"The soul passion is more, more. This is the real want of the soul. We want more of the divine grace, more enlightenment, more faith" (*Our High Calling,* page 188).

Chapter 25

Inviting, Exciting, Igniting a Generation for Christ

"Let the beauty of the Lord our God be upon us,
and establish the work of our hands for us;
Yes, establish the work of our hands."
(Psalm 90:17)

After learning about the eXcite98 program, I decided I had to be there to see what was happening. Before I tell you what happened there, consider another statement about beauty:

The Lord their God will save His people in that day, as a shepherd caring for his sheep. They will shine in his land as glittering jewels in a crown. How wonderful and beautiful all shall be! The abundance of grain and wine will make the young men and girls flourish; they will be radiant with health and happiness (Zechariah 9:16, 17, TLB).

The focus? Beauty and radiance. "Let the beauty of the Lord our God be upon us" (Psalm 90:16). "They looked to Him and were radiant" (Ps. 34:5). And from Zechariah: "Radiant with health and happiness."

This has been a key purpose of this book—to look to Christ, and to become more and more like Him as we reflect His qualities.

God's offerings are exceedingly abundant above all that we could ask or even dream (Ephesians 3:20). What we have sought has been brokenness at the cross, a passion to become Spirit-filled, a passion for God's Word, a passion for the purity found in Christ, a passion for fitness and much more. But as you scan the table of contents you discover that I left out so much: a passion for patience, for tact, for self-control, and many others.

Does that call for a follow-up? More and Still More—Part II?

Chapter 2 of this book—100,000 Spirit-filled Youth—briefly described what the Bible calls the latter rain—an outpouring of God's Spirit similar to what He gave on the Day of Pentecost. The above description of radiant youth comes just before this invitation: "Ask the Lord for rain In the time of the latter rain. The Lord will make flashing clouds; He will give them showers of rain, Grass in the field for everyone" (Zechariah 10:1).

Do you see the connection? First, at the close of Zechariah 9, a promise of youth "radiant with health and happiness." Then, an invitation to ask for the latter rain.

This parallels Joel 2, where God promises to pour His Spirit out on all flesh—sons, daughters, young men, old men, servants, and handmaids (Joel 2:28-30). The terms young men, servants, handmaids seem to indicate young adults, the twenties age group, and also teens—and with old men and all of us, sharing experience and wisdom with young adult enthusiasm.

REPORT ON EXCITE98

Inviting, exciting, igniting. This chapter's title—on a banner that stretched across the front of the La Sierra University Church on August 6-9, 1998—proclaimed the purpose of eXcite98. Here's how the weekend went, and what it portends for the future:

Much, much prayer went into the planning, and prayer was a top priority throughout the weekend

On Thursday morning of the day Excite98 began, Shasta and Jennifer and their team met once again, for the umpteenth time, to pray for God's guidance and blessing. How many should they ask God to send for that night's opening meeting? Maybe one hundred, Shasta thought. No, maybe fifty would be more realistic. Or maybe ten.

How many young adults showed up? More than six hundred. And on Sabbath morning, 1,200 of the 1,800 who packed the La Sierra University Church for Shasta's message were young adults.

The young adults of the church are ready and eager to join efforts to get the three angels' message of Revelation 14 out to "every nation, tribe, tongue and people" of planet earth

On Friday morning Elder Robert Folkenberg, the General Conference president, spent an hour and a half answering questions. He indicated a willingness to have more young adults in leadership positions. He emphasized the importance of proclaiming the second coming of Christ. "Anyone who doesn't have strong convictions about the return of Christ," he said, "might as well become a member of the Rotary Club."

Sabbath evening Pastor Dwight Nelson told of his conviction that the Second Coming is imminent. This generation has become disenchanted with material wealth, he said, and is ready to be quickly mobilized into the army described when Ellen White wrote: "With such an army of workers as our youth, rightly trained, might furnish, how soon the message of a crucified, risen, and soon-coming Saviour might be carried to the whole world! How soon might the end come—the end of suffering and sorrow and sin!" (*Messages to Young People*, page 196).

The audience was diverse in race and interests, and Shasta, Jennifer, and the other leaders arranged for twenty-nine different workshops all designed to enable young adults to use their talents for God. These ranged from Art to Web, with topics such as Bible Studies, Computer Skills, Construction, Health/Exercise, Lesson Design, Organization, Outdoors, and Random Acts.

Shasta and other speakers declared their intention to give themselves totally to Christ and to the work of His church, and almost without exception their listeners made a similar commitment

In her Sabbath morning message Shasta repeatedly asked the 1200 young adults, "Are you in or are you out?" She then said, "If you are in, then give evidence you are in. Make this church a church you can be proud of—one that brings glory to God."

Shasta declared her intention to attend the Andrews University Seminary, starting in the fall of 1998. In May she had been invited to serve as a co-host for

NET '98, where her infectious enthusiasm for God and the church will no doubt bring blessings to listeners on every continent on earth.

My twenty-year-old roommate at eXcite98, Edward Marton, had spent a year helping at the Three Angels' Church in Wichita, Kansas as a Bible worker. Currently he does Bible work in Atlanta, Georgia, and hopes to eventually return to his native Romania, complete ministerial training, and do pastoral work there. As we prayed together, I sensed in him an intense earnestness and sincerity.

I had opportunity to visit with a young couple, Daniel and Yami Bazan, who had just sold everything, purchased a trailer, and are spending the next year traveling from academy to academy to hold weeks of prayer. It is their plan to leave prayer leaders on each campus who can keep a prayer ministry going. They had already lined up more than a half dozen schools that desire this kind of ministry.

THE FUTURE

Before leaving the church campus Saturday night, I went to take a final look at the banner: "eXcite98: Inviting, Exciting, Igniting a Generation for Christ." The challenge is to stay ignited. There below the sign I prayed that God would help each who attended to keep what they had experienced.

Edward and I had a room on the sixth floor of the men's dorm—Sierra Towers—and from our window on the west we could see three crosses someone has placed on a ridge across the street from the library.

These crosses took my thoughts back to the experience I described in my chapter 2 dream: kneeling with a 100,000 Spirit-filled youth and a 100,000 Spirit-filled and totally surrendered leaders and laymen all pressing close to the cross. As I looked at the three crosses in front of the library, I tried to picture all 1,200 young adults kneeling in surrender and commitment before the central cross.

On the flight home I reread most of Roger Morneau's *Incredible Answers to Prayer*. I marked his every reference to the blood of Christ and every reference to intercessory prayer. At the start of chapter 5 he wrote of "prayers sprinkled with the blood of Christ" and of "the mighty power of the Holy Spirit" (page 52). Then on the next page he cited a reference from 1 Timothy 2:1, 2 about "supplications, prayers, intercessions, and giving of thanks for all men."

He put with that a statement from volume 7 of the *Testimonies*—one which pointed out that we don't grasp as we should "the great conflict" that rages continually between "good and evil angels" over every person. I underlined this startling sentence: "We have to meet most powerful adversaries, and it rests with us to determine which shall win" (page 213).

It rests with us to determine which shall win. Mr. Morneau said that at first he thought determining which shall win has to do with the individual. Then he discovered that we can help determine victory or defeat for other persons.

How? The context draws this from the time the early church spent "in prayer and supplication" (Acts 1:14). "We are to find our strength where the early disciples found theirs. 'These all continued with one accord in prayer and supplication' " (Ibid.).

Ever since reading these statements a deepening conviction has gripped me: Whether the 1200 young adults stay ignited rests, at least in part, on whether or not I and others do as 1 Timothy 2:1, 2 instructs: seek God with "supplications, prayers, intercessions, and giving of thanks." For a similar conviction, read again the chapters "A Passion to Pray," and "A Passion to Pray without Ceasing."

Later in his book Mr. Morneau anticipates large numbers of people entering into a prayer ministry for the unsaved. He sees that in the context of this prediction: "Before the final visitations of God's judgments upon the earth there will be among the people of the Lord such a revival of primitive godliness as has not been witnessed since apostolic times" (*The Great Controversy*, page 464).

If not now, when? If not in your heart, whose?

Have you determined to be one who in prayer and in seeking God helps prepare the way for that "revival of primitive godliness"?

For encouragement here again is the pledge of God with which we started: "I promise that I will bless you with everything I have—bless and bless and bless" (Hebrews 6:14, The Message).

"Let us keep our eyes fixed on Jesus, on whom our faith depends from beginning to end" (Hebrews 12:2, TEV). And to close, here's a truth from *Messages to Young People* used three times in my book *30 Days*: "Nothing is apparently more helpless, yet really more invincible, than the soul that feels its nothingness, and relies wholly on the merits of the Saviour" (page 94).

And could I suggest a promise and a comment to write on a 3-by-5 card to keep with you and memorize:

- *"Casting all your care upon Him, for He cares for you"* (1 Peter 5:7).
- *"The relations between God and each soul are as distinct and full as though there were not another soul upon the earth to share His watch care, not another soul for whom He gave His beloved Son"* (Steps to Christ, page 100).

In words given to a comparatively young leader of the past, "Be strong and of good courage" (Joshua 1:6).

Postscript:
Youth On Their Knees

In an earlier book, *Whatever It Takes Praying*, my biggest thrill came from writing the chapter "Jesus Christ—Reason for Enthusiasm." In *30 Days to a More Powerful Prayer Life* the chapter about Jesus, called "Obsessed, Possessed, and Blessed," did the most to awaken a sense of awe. And this book? "A Passion for Oneness With Our Father" stirred me the most. Many times a day I find myself telling my Father, "I love You. I love You."

I love Him for who He is, for His mercy to me, and for what He is doing to raise up Spirit-filled youth. Half the chapters of this book contain testimonies and experiences of youth I know and love. I praise God for each, for they represent the 100,000 praying and Spirit-filled youth that chapter 2 dreams about.

Last week (September 8-12, 1998) Andrews University had 850 teens on campus for the third NAD Teen Prayer and Ministry Conference—with 300 arriving on Tuesday for two days of training as small group leaders, and another 550 coming on Thursday.

A SPIRIT OF PRAYER

The spirit of intercession that pervaded the five days was a foretaste of the latter rain. At every session an invitation was given for up to ten youth to go apart and pray while a message was being given or while study groups were meeting. Twice, more than forty teens responded, and always more than the ten, who then split into smaller groups.

During one session I was praying with a group of five, and a young woman from Bass Academy prayed with such fervor that for a moment I glanced at her. As if bowed before the Father Himself, she moved her hands as she prayed and pleaded for other youth and for NET '98.

After the final session on Saturday night, when most had left the Pioneer Memorial Church, about eighteen youth from Collegedale Academy, with their two sponsors, went to the platform to pray on the very spot where Pastor Dwight would be speaking during NET '98. These were then joined by a dozen from Georgia-Cumberland Academy. I almost wept as I listened to their earnest prayers and as I watched them get into vans for an all-night drive home.

"I had the privilege of attending this conference myself," Pastor Dwight said, "and I am convinced that today's youth represent God's final strategy to conquer this planet through His love. Having been in the midst of these 850 praying young disciples of Jesus and having experienced the power of their intercessory praying, I firmly believe that they are being equipped by the Holy Spirit to infiltrate every level of society with the good news that our Savior is soon to return!"

Amen and Amen!